The Dream Dictionary

Published by Brolga Publishing Pty Ltd
ABN 46 063 962 443
PO Box 12544, A'Beckett St, VIC, 8006, Australia
email: markzocchi@brolgapublishing.com.au

National Library of Australia Cataloguing-in-Publication entry

The dream dictionary / compiled by Lolla Stewart, Paul Bugeja.
2nd ed.
9781921596261 (pbk.)
Dream interpretation--Dictionaries.
Symbolism (Psychology)--Dictionaries.
154.6303

Printed in Indonesia
Cover by David Khan
Typeset by Imogen Stubbs

THE
DREAM
DICTIONARY

A Guide to Understanding
Your Unconscious Mind

With interpretations
by Paul Bugeja and Lolla Stewart

Contents

Foreword

Those who lose dreaming are lost.

AUSTRALIAN ABORIGINAL PROVERB

Before we begin, I need to make something clear—there can be no such thing as a definitive guide to dreams and don't let anyone convince you otherwise!

'What?' I hear you cry. 'I just spent my hard-earned cash buying this book and it's not the be all and end all guide to help me interpret my dreams?'

Relax. You haven't just wasted your money, but the truth is there exist a multitude of theories and explanations about dreams, and just as many different interpretations from any number of sources, built up over the thousands of years we humans have been interested in the meanings behind our dreams.

And, let's not forget, we are all individuals, carrying with us the vastly differing psychological, spiritual, emotional and mental tapestries of our lives, leading to endless possibilities when it comes to the dreamscapes we nightly traverse.

However, as with anything in this often inexplicable life we live—this life of ever unfolding mystery—it is always useful to have at our disposal ways and means by which we can further our understanding:

+ Skills that might allow us to grasp some greater perception of our non-waking life which, despite our best efforts, eludes our ability to comprehend it;

+ Techniques that might help us remember that we have the answers within to solve so many of our own problems, issues and dilemmas;

+ Tools we might find useful to enable us to finally come into our own.

So, what I propose is this.

Think of yourself as an apprentice, ready to learn some basic 'tools of the trade' in an effort to become an investigator and interpreter of your own dreams.

Or, to use a more apt metaphor (get used to metaphor— our dreams are so thick with it that it will become a dreamy, second kind of language to you), you are a dreamer about to be awakened to powers you have forgotten you possess.

Use this guide as a trigger—a way of helping unearth your own forgotten innate ability to interpret your dreams.

I do not in any way propose you take everything I say as gospel or see this book as the ultimate work on dreams and dream interpretation.

Neither would I suggest you go about abruptly changing your life because of what you learn from the pages within.

All I do hope is that this guide might give you the chance to consider your dreams in the way humanity has been doing since time immemorial, and to note down and see what comes of such. Ultimately, it is up to you to decide how important dreams are to you, what they mean and how you apply this information.

For my own part, I will be most satisfied if this book

eventually sits and gathers dust on your shelf.

Why?

Because this will mean you have begun to develop your own ideas and thoughts about dreams and dreaming and no longer require it as a reference...that you have become your own guide, mentor and interpreter.

So read on, dreamer...

Interesting Trivia about Dreams...

+ The word dream stems from the Middle English word, dreme, meaning joy and music.

+ By the age of 60 you will have slept for about 175 000 hours and dreamt for 87 000 hours, during which you will have had 197 000 dreams!

+ Studies show women have more nightmares than men (fearful dreams, confusing dreams and dreams of losing a loved one) and also dream more of family members; have dreams with more negative emotions; experience less physical aggression in their dreams; tend to be more able to recall dreams than men.

+ Men dream more of sex than women (surprise, surprise!)

+ Researchers have found that during REM sleep (for an explanation of REM sleep, see below), males experience erections and females experience increased vaginal blood flow, no matter what the content of the dream. In fact, 'wet dreams' as we know them may not necessarily coincide with overtly sexual dreams.

+ Over 60% of people report recurring dreams.

+ Prior to the 1950's, most people dreamt in black and white, but since then the prevalence of colour dreams has increased, suggesting a possible link to television—nowadays only 12% of people dream exclusively in black and white.

✦ Children and babies have more of the deep sleep required for dreams than do adults—toddlers do not dream about themselves until the age of three or four.

✦ Five minutes after a dream, half the content is forgotten. After ten, this rises to 90%.

✦ Sight impaired people do dream— sounds, tactility and smell are hypersensitive for them. For those who lose sight later in life, some go on to continue having visual dreams.

✦ If you are snoring, you cannot be dreaming.

Dream Theory
and Science

Trust in dreams,
for in them is the hidden gate to eternity.

KAHLIL GIBRAN

Don't be put off by the title of this chapter—it is not going to be filled with lengthy passages of scholarly work requiring a PhD to wade through!

Before we tackle the nuts and bolts of interpretation, a little history on the various theories proposed over the ages about dreams and a few scientific facts on sleep and dreaming will help give you some perspective on how deeply dreaming permeates our lives.

It will be quick and painless, hopefully even interesting!

For millennia we have pondered the meaning of our dreams. In nearly every culture there are records of dream keeping and interpretation which have right up until today built up a bank of possibilities as to why it is we dream, and what these dreams might mean.

The remarkable thing about dreams is that they seem to traverse both the physical and metaphysical realms, and in doing so have sparked generation after generation of scholarly, spiritual and philosophical enquiry into their meaning.

The Ancients—the Dreamer and Other Realms of Existence

It is easy to forget Australia lays claim to the earliest race to incorporate dreaming as an essential part of its cultural fabric—the Aboriginals and their 'Dreamtime'.

This race has the longest continuous cultural history of any group of people on Earth, dating back 65 000 years. While the Dreamtime has a much broader frame of reference in terms of the totality of Aboriginal spirituality, dreaming is seen as a kind of 'spiritual walkabout' for the indigenous peoples of Australia. Yet, rather than psychoanalyse dreams as Western society is caught up in doing, Australia's aboriginals ask the simple questions of 'who, when and where?' to work out the meaning of their dreams.

The earliest physical attempt at recording dreams dates back to 3000BC when the ancient Sumerians of Mesopotamia, the cradle of civilisation, transcribed their dreaming onto clay tablets, most often cited through the Epic of Gilgamesh.

Majorly concerned with divination, the Mesopotamians believed that the soul, or some part of it, left the body while one was sleeping to visit places and persons. As it travelled on its nightly journey the soul could glean important information about the future, carried along the way by the

Goddess of Dreams, Ningal.

The Egyptians also held dreams in high esteem, believing they were potentially the key to the future, and also a way to communicate with the Gods, were a form of divine magic, were able to cure illness and, in the case of nightmares, could wreak havoc upon one's enemies.

To this day there are numerous examples of dream recordings in hieroglyphs in still-standing Egyptian ruins. The Dream Book is one—a papyrus containing dream examples and interpretations—and is believed to date back to the early reign of Ramesses I. Dreams of royalty were given special attention with temples called Serapeums, named after Serapis the god of dreams, built to 'incubate' dreams in. Before entering these temples, the dreamer usually underwent various procedures, including cleansing, purging, and the offering up of prayer, in order to experience the desired dream.

In the Greek and Roman eras, dreams were viewed as direct messages from the gods or from the dead, providing solutions to all manner of things—dream interpreters even accompanied military leaders into battle to help with strategy. The Helllenistic period (320-150 BC) saw the main focus of dreams centre around healing, with temples called Asclepieions built for those with illnesses to spend time in and incubate dreams that could shed light on curing their ills.

The ancient Hebrews believed dreams were a direct connection with God. Solomon, Nebuchednezzar, Jacob, and most famously of all, Joseph (he of the technicolour coat) were all visited in dreams.

Dream incubation was also prevalent in Hebrew culture.

Hisda, a Babylonian of the third century, decreed that every dream (except those occurring during fasting) meant something and was said to proclaim that 'a dream not interpreted, is like a letter unread'. This found its way into the Talmud, the famous collection of oral rabbinical teachings from the period 200-500 AD, which became the basis for many rabbinic legal codes and customs, and includes over 200 references to dreams.

The Chinese considered the dreamer's soul (the hun) to leave the body at night and visit the dead, and in India, the Sacred Books of Wisdom (Vedas) were written between1500 and 1000 BC. Contained within the Vedas was lengthy discussion on dreams and their interpretations.

Native Americans have long held the belief that, through ritual, spiritual dreams can be incubated and thus wisdom and guidance for life can be obtained. Vision quests, involving ritualistic behaviour, fasting, sleep deprivation, isolation, and even self-inflicted pain were undertaken, following which the tribe's shaman or medicine man would be called upon to interpret the dream's message.

And of course there are the famous dreamcatchers, an authentic American Indian tradition intended to protect the sleeping individual. The specific design of the dreamcatcher allows the positive dreams to slip through the hole in the centre and glide down the feathers to the sleeping person below. The negative dreams would get caught in the web and dissipate when the first rays of the sun struck them.

While these have become a common tourist memento amongst today, their powers are still held in firm belief by their original creators.

Modern Times—Science Meets Spirituality

Post antiquity, dreams began to lose their significance as Western culture (and, by virtue of this, Christianity) began to dominate during the Middle Ages. Dreams came to be considered in the context of their relationship to God or, with the case of nightmares, to the devil, evil spirits and possession.

Even this consideration of dreams was set aside as society became more structured and science began to surface as a dominant force. By the Industrial Age dreams were mere flights of fancy, explored fictitiously by writers and poets, and only taken seriously by 'heathens' or the supposedly 'less developed' and thus supposedly less enlightened peoples of the world.

Then, a man came along to change all this—the great psychoanalyst, Sigmund Freud.

Seeing dreams as a mirror of the psyche's content, Freud essentially revived some of the key ideas of the ancients, claiming that dream content was linked to our waking life, calling dreams 'the royal road to the unconscious'. In his landmark work of 1899, The Interpretation of Dreams, he wrote that dreams were the undisguised fulfilment of repressed wishes, desires and motivations, and argued they should only be investigated and interpreted by a psychotherapist. Heavily interwoven into his theory was the belief that dreams were inextricably linked to sexual themes, an assertion which later led various aspects of his theory discredited.

Freud's famous contemporary, Carl Jung, restored some balance to Freudian theory by bringing 'the spiritual' back into the dream equation. When he retired in his eighties he had interpreted over 80 000 dreams and come to the conclusion that there existed universality across the many dreamers and dreams with which he had worked.

His most stunning conclusion?

That the individual, through careful recording and observation, was in fact the best interpreter of his or her own dreams. In the end Jung held he had no real theory on dreams, but rather that each and every person who meditates on their dreams will find something useful in them and the thoughts and feelings they evoked.

A wide range of dream theories emerged in the wake of Freud and Jung's seminal studies, but the next most important turning point came in the 1950s.

Nathaniel Kleitman, often referred to as the father of modern sleep research, made a startling discovery. In his sleep laboratory he witnessed the eyes of sleepers making fast movements, which he went on to title 'rapid eye movement', or REM. With careful observation he came to the conclusion that it was during this REM sleep that people seemed to dream.

At the same time as Kleitman was making his discoveries, Calvin Hall developed a cognitive theory based on over 50 000 dream reports, further supporting Jung's theories, and went on to posit that meaningful predictions could be made about a dreamer's behaviour and lifestyle from careful study of their dreams. Dement and Fisher followed this up with controlled experiments in the 1960s which went on to show that psychological wellbeing could conceivably be linked to dreaming.

These landmark theories of the mid-twentieth century

were the predecessors to many more over the next 20 years, some carrying weight, others more questionable in their veracity. For example, in the 1980s Crick and Mitchinson used the analogy of the cortex as being something like a computer which needs to go offline each day to prevent it overloading and to 'debug' itself. According to their theory, this happens during REM sleep, and yet if we follow the analogy—if dreaming is indeed a kind of mental debugging process—we should in fact therefore NOT try to remember our dreams, rather letting all this material go so that cortex is clear and ready for activity during the next waking day. This is clearly something that goes against the grain of so many other theories which encourage remembering dreams that it has since been called into question in terms of its validity.

Other conjecture abounds and continues to be presented by the scientific community, but there is still no consensus as to why we dream and what purpose dreams serve. The only thing that researchers for the most agree upon from the evidence accumulated over the past

50 years is that dreams are coherent and do relate somehow to previous waking experiences.

A Little Dream Science—The Sleep Cycle.

To better understand what takes place in the dreaming mind we need to have a basic understanding of the sleep cycle.

There are four distinct sleep stages and every human goes through several cycles of these in a typical night. The most vivid dreams, and those most likely to be remembered in the morning, occur during REM sleep, but dreams may occur at any of the four stages:

+ Stage 1: REM sleep, generally occurring from 90-100 minutes after the initial onset of sleep, during which blood pressure rises and the heart rate and respiration speed up. Voluntary muscles also become paralysed.
+ Stage 2: A light sleep, characterised by non-rapid eye movements, during which the muscles are relaxed and the heart rate slows, preparing the body for deep sleep.
+ Stags 3 and 4: Feature non-rapid eye movement, during which the body enters into a very deep sleep, with stage four the deepest sleep we can experience.

All four stages repeat throughout the sleep period, generally occurring between four and seven times per night. Sometimes we remember dreams from earlier in the night, but in most cases the dreams that are remembered are those that occur closest to waking. Through their work with volunteers who agreed to be awakened constantly during REM sleep, researchers know that dreaming occurs during all four to seven sessions of REM sleep, with those awakened during REM sleep generally providing very vivid descriptions of their dreams.

While scientists have as yet not been unable to develop a means of capturing dream content direct from the brain, new scanning technologies being developed in the USA are moving at such a pace that it might eventually become possible to record the actual brainwaves of sleepers and in doing so capture their dreams, just like a movie—your dreams, coming to a cinema near you!

But we dreamers can't wait for that – so let's do what we can ourselves, now.

How to Remember and Record Your Dreams

Your vision will become clear
Only when you look into your heart.
Who looks outside, dreams.
Who looks inside, awakens.

CARL JUNG

Now that you've had a chance to read and understand a little of the history and theory of dreams and their interpretation, the real work begins. It's time to develop your own theory.

Yes, develop your own theory.

The best kind of dream theory is that which you devise for yourself—and you don't need to be an ancient Greek scholar, Native American shaman or psychoanalyst to do so.

Like most theories, you can only develop your own through some careful work and research. Reading this book and no doubt others like it is a good start. But for all the theories and ideas and such, there can be no denying that dreams are an intrinsically personal part of each and every one of us, coming from deep within our souls/unconsciousness, and thus we as individuals have the power to work out exactly what they mean.

In saying this I am in no way proposing that you discount or write off the way dreams have been interpreted and pondered over the ages. Quite the opposite in fact as initially we need prompts, reminders and suggestions about how to make our way through our dreams and work out what they mean, which is why a guide to dreams like this one can be useful.

First things first though—you need to 'capture' your dreams so that you have material to work with.

How do I record dreams?

As the great philosopher Goethe proclaimed 'Whatever you can do or dream you can, begin it. Boldness has genius, power, and magic in it. Begin it now.'

And beginning this dream interpretation process is simple.

First and foremost, the obvious—you need the right equipment with which to record your dreams.

This can be as simple as a paper notepad and pen or something more elaborate, like a bound diary and a fountain pen you keep only for the dream diary. I would recommend the latter. Remember, the dream material you put into this diary is precious, so why not have it kept somewhere special and recorded with an implement specially set aside for the purpose?

Divide each page of the diary down the middle so that on one side you can transcribe the actual dreams and on the other you can interpret the meanings. You may like to even use a different coloured pen when you start the interpreting as such might so act as a visual cue to your brain that there are going to be two quite different sets of information in the diary.

Rather than dividing down the middle, you could use opposing pages so that you allow enough room for full interpretations—as you will see below, there is a lot of material to consider in your dreams and you may find you end up with more information in the interpretation than in the actual dream itself.

With this in mind, an alternative is to keep a separate diary for your interpretations which will not restrict you in how deep and detailed you wish to go.

Bottom line, there is no right or wrong—do whatever you feel is going to be best for you!

For the internet-generation there are an array of online dream diaries and dream blogs where you can record your dreams and access resources to help interpret them.

However, if you decide to go down this path, it would still make sense to keep a good old fashioned paper version also.

Why?

Think about it. You wake up in the morning and your head is crowded with fragments of dreams…you might even wake up in the middle of the night, quite often in the thick of some amazing dreamscape…but as vibrant and intense and incredible as the dream was, it very quickly seeps away as the cold hard light of reality slips in.

Consequently, accessibility to the diary is paramount—you need it right there, within reach, ready to have scrawled down in it everything you can remember of your dreams. Of course, some of us are a little better and more clearheaded on waking and thus able to get down our dreams clearly and concisely...others wake up a little less able!

For this latter set of dreamers, an alternative to writing is to vocally record your dreams. Dictaphones are easily come buy and not too expensive, quite a few mobile phones have a voice recorder function on them and digital music devices like iPods also have the capacity to attach a simple recording device that will allow you to record memos.

This method of catching your dreams can be quite valuable. Speaking the dreams out aloud is potentially a stimulus to reactivate them, with some studies having shown that retelling your dreams to someone else as having the possibility of unearthing dream moments not previously recalled.

It is also potentially a much quicker and more accurate mind 'dump' of your dreams, much in the same way that stream of consciousness exercises allow people to reveal things about themselves they might not otherwise. Clearly, you can speak much faster than you can write, and speaking requires less concentration than writing, so this could be the most effective way to get everything out as quickly as you can upon waking and thus not to miss out on any precious dream material.

This isn't, however, to let you off the hook of actually writing your dreams out! Rather, later during the day you should listen back over the recording and transcribe it into your dream diary, giving you another opportunity to maybe remember more of your dreams and delve even further into the detail and possible interpretation.

What do I record?

In a nutshell, EVERYTHING.

The more material you have, the better. Also, generally speaking, the more often you record your dreams, the more details you will recall and the more meaning you will be able to extract from them.

Some basic tips to bear in mind when recording your dreams:

1. Try and write down the series of dreams over the night in the order they occurred. Initially you may not be able to find meaning in this order, but as you hone your dream analysis skills, relationships between the dreams will start to become apparent and important.

2. When characters and places appear, be really aware of who/what they are and how closely they resemble people or places you know.

3. Record all non-human and inanimate objects, even if they seem obscure at the time, as they are potentially likely to have quite significant symbolic meaning.

4. Highlight recurring events or characters, and note where possible the subtle or larger difference each time the dream recurs.

5. Note down striking colours that appear in your dreams, most especially when people or things are not the colour they usually are.

6. Most importantly of all, carefully monitor and record any emotions the dream has evoked in you.

How you actually feel after a dream, especially straight afterwards, is one of the most powerful keys to interpretation. Dreams give us a safe area to express emotions which might be difficult to release in our waking lives, so the emotions we take from our dreams are an important part of working through what the dreams mean and how they connect to our consciousness. Make it a priority as soon as you open your dream diary to record how the dream made you feel, both while you were dreaming and also as you woke out of it.

How do I remember my dreams?

One of the most common complaints from people who want to start the dream interpretation process is 'But I never remember my dreams' or 'I only ever remember bits of my dreams but never much' or 'I forget them as soon as I forget them as soon as I wake up' etc...

There is no doubt that some people do have issues remembering their dreams and even believe they don't dream at all. The main barrier to recall is that dreaming is predominantly a right brain activity.

To explain, the right brain is visual, processing information in an intuitive and simultaneous way, looking first at the whole picture then the details.

On the other hand, the left brain is verbal and processes information in an analytical and sequential way, looking first at the pieces then putting them together to get the whole.

Thus, we dream in the right brain where the information is metaphorical, which becomes difficult for the left brain to grapple with logically and literally upon waking.

This is why recording dreams or writing them down

immediately upon waking is essential so that the left brain is activated simultaneously and can create narratives and memories based on the nightly right brain dreaming.

However, the key to recalling your dreams lays in the most fundamental aspect of dreaming—sleeping well!

Sounds pretty obvious maybe, but how can you expect to dream and remember your dreams unless you get a good night's sleep? Studies have shown that insomniacs and poor sleepers dream less and recall dreams less, potentially linked to depression and other mental illnesses.

So, it is important to get your sleeping right and thus get your dreaming right. Just in the way so many ancient cultures practiced dream incubation, which was essentially a method to prepare oneself for sleep and dreaming, you too can improve your sleep and the dreams that come with it. Try not to eat or drink anything too much before sleep as this stimulates both your nervous and digestive systems, and absolutely stop watching TV or sitting at your computer screen or reading a book reasonably well in advance of sleep.

You need to be in as relaxed as state as possible, with a calm mind that is open to peaceful, deep slumber.

As you lay in bed and feel sleep starting to tug you towards unconsciousness, hold the questions about your life at the moment clearly in your mind and, as you drift off to sleep, ask yourself to have dreams that will help you find answers to your questions and to remember them in the morning. This simple but powerful suggestion will hopefully stimulate your right brain in its dream state and your left brain upon waking.

The opposite end of the night, waking, is also important. Try where possible to wake naturally without an alarm clock or other outside intervention, and with enough time to take note of your dreams and feelings. A glass of water by your bedside is the perfect way to re-hydrate your body upon waking and, believe it or not, is as good a stimulant as a hit of caffeine!

Sound like 'hocus pocus' or silly psychological nonsense?!

Dare you to try it—you might be very surprised with the outcome.

The fact that you are now actively trying to recall your dreams upon waking should also act as a 'brain flexing' mechanism to ally your waking mind more closely with your dream experiences.

Some helpful hints about dream recall:

1. You've really got to want to recall your dreams. This can't be done in a half-baked, unbelieving manner. The more you believe, the more likely it is you will remember.

2. Dream recall is an inbuilt function of your brain. Man has been recalling his dreams for thousands of years and thus it is an inherent human trait. So, just like exercising your body, exercising your brain to recall dreams will help you get 'dream-recall-fit' again and more able to remember them.

3. Read over your dream diary before bed. This will help you get in touch with your dream-life and prepare you for the night ahead.

4. If you awaken during the night, try not to move from the position you're lying in as this will disturb your

dream-state, making it difficult to return to. If you must move to get more comfortable (or because your partner is suddenly hogging the bed!), consider writing down whatever you can recall of the broken dream before you find your new sleep position.

5. Most importantly of all, don't stress about recall! You dream every night, many times a night, and you will remember what you must when you should. Stressing out about the fact that you aren't having any luck with recall or that your recall is not improving will only make matters worse.

The key point to remember is that, as scientifically proven, everyone dreams and the reality is anyone can improve their dream recall ability, including you!

Interpreting Your Dreams

Some men see things as they are and ask why.
Others dream things that never were
and ask why not.

GEORGE BERNARD SHAW,
IRISH PLAYWRIGHT AND CRITIC

Being chased

Running slowly on the spot

FALLING

Arriving late to something important

Someone alive being dead or vice versa

Flying

EMBARRASSING ONESELF IN PUBLIC

Not being able to see or focus properly

Going to the toilet

Snakes

BEING NAKED IN PUBLIC...

S ound familiar?

I'd place money on the fact that you have had at least one, if not several, dreams containing some of these things at some point in your life.

Although not an exhaustive list, these are some of the most common dreams recorded.

Such commonality leads to the conclusion that there exists across all dreamers and dreamscapes the ability to interpret dreams—there are specific and shared meanings that we can all relate to, and from these hopefully learn something about ourselves and our lives.

At this point it is important to reiterate once more the most important thing you can learn from this book—that dream meanings themselves are intrinsically linked to the dreamer and thus best interpreted by individually.

Despite what Freud might have liked us to believe (he was entitled to make a buck I guess), you are the best interpreter of your own dreams as they are ultimately an important communication about you and your life from one part of your 'self' to the other—from your subconscious to conscious self.

Thus, ultimately it is your gut feeling you should trust when it comes to understanding your dreams. However, a guide like this is a way of nudging the dormant power you have within to interpret your dreams and to reconnect with your own intuitive ability to look inside them, relate them to your waking life and have them help you in some way.

Following from this, no matter how in tune with yourself you are or how long you go on to actively interpret your dreams, it's rare that you will immediately understand them and there is a very specific reason for this.

As already discussed, your right brain is active while dreaming whereas, upon awakening, the left brain 'kicks in' to allow you to slip from your dream state into 'reality'. (Imagine if this didn't happen—we wouldn't know the difference between dreams and reality and could potentially suffer from permanent psychosis!)

This is why it is important to write down as much dream material as you can upon waking to get out all the right brain metaphorical material which your left brain (in conjunction with your right brain) can sort through and make sense of.

Having said this, it's important to remember that you will often not be looking for literal meaning in your dreams. Quite the contrary, your chief task is to work through metaphor. What you need to do is extract the meaning of the dream from its action, in effect deciphering the meaning of the dream from its superficial content.

This is easier than it sounds, believe it or not, because you will remember the parts of the dream that are most important to you and, once these are written down, you will then be able to go on and identify what strikes you most strongly about them.

In summary, the basic question you need to consider is not what the dream is about in its simple obvious rendering to you while you sleep, but how it relates to your waking life.

Where to Start

So, you've got your dream diary before you with a dream written out in as much detail as possible.

What now?

There are two levels, of equal importance, at which to interpret the dream—you must consider both the overall dream itself and the more intricate details contained within it.

The Big Picture

First we need to start 'big' and look at the dream as a whole before going on to concentrate on the details and the symbology that goes them. Reading over the dream a few times will hopefully help you identify its main theme or concept also how you feel about it.

The easiest way to do this is via an example.

You awaken one morning and record a very detailed, adventurous dream where you travel through amazing landscapes—places you've never seen before with strange people and objects encountered along the way. You never quite get to your destination, even though you know you are heading somewhere in particular.

There are clearly going to be any number of symbolic meanings to the more detailed components of this dream—the strange red dog that is accompanying you; the green sky, which suddenly turns purple; the yellow cap you are wearing, even though you have never owned a cap in your life; your mother being the bus driver; a vampire sitting next to you, telling you her life story while sucking the juice from a tomato.

Stripping all this back, thematically in this dream there is the notion of searching for something and not being able to pin down what it is, no matter how long or hard you search. For some, feelings of frustration or maybe hopelessness might come with this kind of endless searching and travelling dream...conversely, for others, feelings of exhilaration and wonder could come from this endless, exciting search. Both are equally valid interpretations and illustrate how important it is for the dreamer to somehow define the theme of the dream and the feelings that go with it for them personally before digging into deeper detailed interpretations of the dream's components.

Now you need to go on and match the theme, concept and feelings to your life.

So, following on with the example, what are you currently searching for that is either causing you frustration or excitement? A new job? Home? Relationship? Even something as innocuous as a new car?! It could be one of many things, but clearly for it to have meaning it must be directly relatable to you and your current life.

Once you've made the connection, the answer will not necessarily directly present itself and you may still struggle with the interpretation, and how to apply it to your life. However, you can now go on with at least a little clearer understanding of your current life questions and take this with you each night into your dreams where eventually (hopefully!) the answers will present themselves. This is where the concept of recurring dreams is fascinating and potent.

When a dream recurs over and over we should consider such as a form of our subconscious advertising to us that we are not dealing with a certain aspect of our life, potentially blocking us from moving forward or growing more in terms of self awareness and development. If we can identify the theme of this recurring dream, and what it relates to, we at least have the information about this life 'roadblock' and can take some action to remove it from our path ahead.

The Devil (or Angel!) is in the Details

Whereas identifying the theme and the feeling of our dreams gives us the framework and overall interpretation, many of the small details can also hold meanings, offering a deeper and more profound insight into what our dreams are trying to tell us.

Ultimately, as stressed earlier, the specifics of your life and who you are as a person will often dictate the symbols behind the material that appears in your dreams. Each of us will carry our own set of associations, imperative to interpretation.

However, using a dream dictionary, especially during

the early stages of dream interpretation, is a great way to open yourself to the possibility of what things might mean when they appear in your dreams. Dictionaries give the most common definitions for particular items, from which you can go on to work out exactly what your dreams mean for you personally, and, if you subscribe to Jungian theory, there is a vast crossover in this symbology from person to person, culture to culture. Thus, don't be surprised when more often than not the interpretations in this guide fall in line very closely with your own intuition about what individual things symbolise in your dreams. Also be prepared that sometimes they won't, and it's important for you to go with your instincts and interpret as you see fit.

In the interpretations section you will find an alphabetical listing of meanings, by no means exhaustive, but which should contain a fairly solid cross-representation of the things that appear in your dreams. As well as the very specific meanings in the dictionary, certain groups of things also alert us to a particular aspect of our life or self that our dreams are pointing to.

Some of the more obvious groupings include:

✦ Animals, which often symbolise specific traits, good and bad. Domesticated animals are linked to traits you have more control over, whereas wild animals point to the traits you find it harder to manage. Animals are also linked to your instinctive and emotional nature and can also have more specific meanings

✦ Modes of transportation, which reflect both the direction in which you are heading and also might have some relation to issues with your body (ie your body as the vehicle/mode of transportation for your soul)

✦ Colours, which all have very specific meanings that can be overlaid with other specific symbolic interpretation to find deep understanding of the overall dream (they are not listed individually in the interpretation section, but rather under 'colours')

✦ Clothing, which often represents your moods and state of mind

✦ Weather and climatic elements, which generally symbolise powerful emotions and change

✦ Types of rooms you are in or pass through, which suggest the portion of your ego the dream is about. For example, a basement as the subconscious, the bedroom as relationships and the unconscious, the kitchen as self nourishment etc

✦ Directions, with forwards and backwards representing movements in time; upwards representing the spiritual or intellectual and downwards the grounded and physical; left referring to the emotional and creative part of ourselves, right to the logical and reasoned.

The more you go on to interpret your dreams, the more intuitive will become your own understanding of these kinds of groupings and the myriad of specific meanings the details of your dreams symbolise.

Use the interpretation section of this guide as much as you need to initially, but over time start to take stabs at what your dreams mean, only coming back to the general interpretations when you are particularly stumped over the meaning of something for which you have no genuine intuitive response.

Bringing it all together.

Bringing the bigger picture and the finer details together is the true craft of anyone trying to delve more deeply into dream interpretation.

Something which might help you with this is to approach dreams the way I do.

I like to think of dreams as being similar to a movie, maybe specifically a 3-D one!

Think about it. There you are, in the audience, wrapped up in the dark, sitting back and watching the movie playing before you, and yet somehow you are drawn right into the action, with things coming at you left, right and centre.

The movie has a particular theme or genre which you're vaguely aware of and an overarching story that you are putting together as you watch it, but within this there are many individual elements you can identify—actors (you're usually one of them), the scenes and settings, the props and costumes, and of course the action and plot.

And, importantly of course, the film makes you feel a certain way—you go on an emotional rollercoaster ride with the character you associate most with, the protagonist (being you, of course!)

Deconstructing dreams down to these elements in this format might just be the key you're looking for, so go ahead and try it. But there are no rules—make up your own analogy for dreaming if it helps and apply it.

Just do it, and do it now, so that you can start this important process of interpretation and the potential for wonderful revelation that comes with it. As you commit yourself to interpreting and understanding your dreams you will develop your own personal style and framework within which to do so.

The key to this whole adventure of interpretation is to have faith in yourself and your own powers of delving into your dreams and understanding their meaning...

Nightmares and Prophecies

Could we but mould our dreams at will,
And keep them free from harm or ill,
How pleasant it would be,
To deem our waking hours but dreams,
And that, our life which now but seems
A baseless fantasy.

LADY M. W. MONTAGUE

t would be remiss not to briefly mention two elements of dreams that especially fascinate people—nightmares and prophetic dreams.

Nightmares

In the past considered the product of being possessed by evil spirits or incubi (known as mare or *mære* in old English), nightmares have plagued and intrigued us for as long as dreams have.

Essentially, these are nothing more than dreams which evoke a particular emotional response, typically fear and anxiety, containing content we find particularly disturbing in our waking lives infecting our sleeping lives. given their extreme content and the emotional resonance they leave with us upon waking. Given their extreme content and the emotional resonance they leave with us upon waking, nightmares often leave a lasting impression on us in their aftermath.

But if we hold true that dreams are a message from the best part of ourselves—from the part that wants to help us move forward in the direction of our desires and wants and aspirations, towards realising our waking dreams—nightmares come for good reason and with good intent despite the way they make us feel at the time.

Dream analysts contend that nightmares come to help us fix something about ourselves that might harm us if not dealt with, thus acting as a mirror to the darker side of our souls and the less pleasant things about ourselves that we must face up to.

In line with this, a frequent theme of nightmares is being pursued by a malicious person or monster, indicating some aspect of our emotional life we are running away from. This can turn into a recurring dream, indicative of a need to face up to the monster and 'slay' it or expel it, thus also facing up to that part of ourselves we are avoiding.

Other frequent nightmares include being held hostage, drowning or suffocating, and being paralysed. The meanings of these are metaphorical yet literal—maybe you feel as though someone at your workplace is 'holding you hostage' and not allowing you to work to best affect? Is your partner overwhelming you and not allowing you enough time for yourself, and thus suffocating you? Are you experiencing a particularly stressful time with too much to do and therefore feel unable to do any of them properly, essentially paralysed?

A simple method of dealing with nightmares is to arm

yourself before sleep with the means to tackle them. As you interpret and analyse the elements of the nightmare and how it relates to your life, take the solutions with you into your dreams with a positive will to face up to the problem both in your dreams and in your waking life.

Persistent nightmares, however, could be an indication of deep-seated issues which might best be dealt with in a formal therapy environment. If your sleep is consistently disturbed in this way, you could consider seeking the help of a health professional.

Prophetic dreams

The notion of dreams being prophetic has been around since ancient times with many early cultures (as indicated earlier) believing in the possibility of dreams being a key to revealing the future.

There are also sufficient documented cases of people dreaming of and predicting the future for there to be some merit in dreams potentially being prophetic, although, of course, there is no way too actually verify this.

Edgar Cayce, often referred to as the father of the New Age Movement and a psychic of great renown, has his own string of theories about dreams. Given his immersion in all things spiritual, he purported that there was the possibility that dreams might furnish some clues as to the future, either specifically or symbolically.

He also held that that dreams are also potentially a

conveyance of direct connection to the spiritual world—a conduit to God. (It should be noted that he rounded out his dream theory with a more psychological bent, also believing that dreams could paint a symbolic picture of one's current life and present solutions to problems, much more in line with other prominent dream theorists of the twentieth century.)

Some famous examples of prophetic dreams include:

+ Joan of Arc predicting her death
+ Abraham Lincoln dreaming of his own death just days before his assassination
+ The defeat of Napoleon at Waterloo being foretold
+ Robert Louis Stevenson getting ideas for many of his best stories, including *Dr Jekyll and Mr Hyde*
+ Paul McCartney hearing the melody of *Yesterday*
+ Einstein conceiving the theory of relativity in a dream
+ Elias Howe seeing through to the design of the sewing machine in a dream (he dreamt of Indians chasing him with spears that had holes in the heads, which helped him conceive of the hole being in the sharp end of the needle rather than the blunt)
+ Jack Nicklaus improving his golf swing (after dreaming of a new way to hold his club)

One contemporary theory about dreams and their potential prophetic nature suggests our brains are so powerful that dreams are in fact the subconscious way of guessing at the future. By bringing together everything it knows about the individual's past and present and the likely outcomes of any actions he or she might take given this, the brain takes a stab at what will happen, which is essentially prophetic.

Another theory purports that, given we only use about 10% of our brains, the remaining 90% contains something like a roadmap to our lives, which we occasionally have the power to cross over into and gain some knowledge of through our dreams (with the concept of déjà vu linked also to this.)

For the purposes of this book, I would offer the simple observation that whether your dreams are prophetic or not remains something for you to ascertain…and something you might be able to gather more information on if you keep a good enough dream diary.

Find Your Own Meaning:

The Great Challenge

Dreaming permits each and every one of us
To be quietly and safely insane every night
of our lives.

WILLIAM DEMENT

Although it may sound as if I'm trying to do myself out of a job, in recording and interpreting your dreams, your aim should be to ultimately put together your own dictionary of definitions.

This is actually easier than it sounds.

It will require a little more work than just keeping a dream diary and using the interpretations in this guide because you will need to keep a 'non-dream' diary also. This journal can be as simple or detailed as you wish and time permits, but at the least it should be a record of daily events in your life, especially those of particular note, and importantly, how you are feeling about life at the time of them happening.

Give yourself a year and then start to read back over your dream diary and the interpretations within it. Look for the common themes your dreams seem to follow and the associated meanings. Pinpoint particular people, places or things that appear in your dreams and consider the context in which they appear.

Simultaneously compare these to what was actually happening in your life by looking through your other journal—you will of course have already been considering such anyway on a daily basis as you interpret your dreams. Having a year's worth of material to pour back over will reveal even more to you than it did fresh at the time of recording it.

This self reflection, both during your waking and sleeping life, is one of the most powerful tools for personal and spiritual growth you can possibly hold. I highly recommend it as path towards a happier and more productive existence—a life where you can take responsibility for yourself and the path you are on, solving your own problems with the wisdom you ultimately have within you (whether you're aware of it or not!)

Good luck dreamer—sleep tight, dream deep and awaken (and write down your dreams!), refreshed and ready for the day ahead and the joys and challenges it will bring...

Interpretations

A man's dreams are an index to his greatness.

ZADOK RABINWITZ

Abandonment

Being abandoned, especially by someone you trust, can reflect fears you have about a strong relationship in your life. It may also indicate you are relying on the strength or wisdom of someone else, which makes you feel vulnerable. On an internal level, it may symbolise an aspect of your personality that is not helping you.

In a positive light, however, just as every loss is an opportunity to gain something new, abandonment can be, in fact, the beginning of finding your own strength.

Abduction

Feeling at the mercy of something or someone who has all the power, as in being abducted, can be symbolic of things being out of control in your work, relationships or some other aspect

A

of your life. What you perhaps experience as frustration in your waking life may become full-blown terror in this dream. It is the subconscious reminding you of how much is at stake when your self-fulfilment is thwarted.

Abortion

An abortion can represent plans which fail to come to fruition. It may also indicate you are cut off from your inner child and are uncomfortable with playfulness and the aspects of yourself that demand attention.

In terms of your subconscious, abortion could be seen as a warning that you are not ready to accept the repercussions of what you hope for or have put in motion.

Accident

A crash in a vehicle of some kind can indicate things are in danger of coming to an abrupt halt— perhaps you are on a collision course with someone at work or in your relationships.

Essentially, it is your subconscious warning you to be more careful.

Whatever it is that you crash into, the suddenness of stopping indicates the direction you are taking comes into contact with a strong oppositional force that can change everything in a second. If injuries result from the accident, this can warn of long-term repercussions.

Actor/Actress

The idea of playing a role is symbolised in a dream character who is an actor or actress. Perhaps you are aware of pretence or deception on your own or another's part, or a need to please a critical audience.

This may also indicate that some aspect of your life is out of touch with reality and that you are wearing a mask. Dreaming of being in a play and forgetting your lines indicates anxiety about performing to others' expectations.

Airplane

A plane as a vehicle for rising into the sky may symbolise your desire to reach new heights in your profession, or your consciousness.

If the plane is landing smoothly, it may indicate the successful completion of a period of striving, or personal desires being fulfilled— a rough landing or a crash can symbolise the danger of some of your plans and the difficulty in getting them to come to fruition safely.

If you have a literal fear of flying and have a trip planned, a dream of a plane crash should not be taken as pre-cognitive. It is merely the grip of your fear working out as you sleep.

Airport

As an airport is the venue for departures and arrivals, this usually symbolises beginnings or some sort or a reunion. It may be your personal hopes and goals taking wings, or the commencement of a new relationship.

If you are meeting someone at the airport, this could

A

mean that a big transition has been made and aspects of your life, formerly separated, are coming together.

Alcohol

Others drinking alcohol indicates they are out of control, with the alcohol being an excuse for their behaviour, essentially meaning they are not in a condition to help you in some way that you need help at present.

If you dream of yourself consuming alcohol, it may indicate you are searching for an excuse to do something out of the ordinary or to avoid performing some normal task you have before you.

Angel

As angels in mythology are always associated with a message from a higher realm and warnings or announcements of blessings, an angel appearing in a dream is a symbol of your higher consciousness alerting you to an important message or lesson to learn. This is a call to study the dream itself carefully, as well as your life circumstances, to discover what it is that you really must learn.

Animals

(see individual animals for the meanings)

Antiques

Old furniture and décor in a dream house can symbolise

thing that are beautiful and priceless from the past.

It may also represent all that is valuable in your heritage or family background.

If they are dust-covered or damaged, the dream may convey some neglect of these important things. A negative feeling about the antiques in your dream can indicate you are feeling trapped by your past.

Ants

Ants in a dream are an indication of good business activity, generally due to your ability to cooperate with others to achieve your desires.

They also point towards feelings of general activity in most areas of your life.

Apron

Wearing an apron can be a symbol of motherhood, or needing to be nurtured.

Alternatively, it can also symbolise a barrier between you and your inner Mother.

A male dreaming of an apron can interpret this as indicating a feeling of being tied to a real maternal figure, or dominated by the inner Mother in an unhealthy way.

Attacks

Struggling with an attacker can be a symbol of the feelings of threat you experience in family, friendships or profes-

A

sional life.

The outcome of the attack indicates the inner weakness or strength you believe you have.

Emerging victorious represents your subconscious' resilience in the face of challenge, while falling victim can show that you lack the self-belief to win.

Avalanche

Dreaming of an avalanche you are unable to flee is a signifier of some kind of stress in a life situation which is controlling you.

Fleeing the danger and watching it from safety tends to indicate that you are managing the stress while performing your normal duties and functions.

B

Baby

Where you are not pregnant or a new parent, the appearance of a dream baby can symbolise new beginnings in professional or personal life.

A new project requiring a lot of time and attention can be reflected in dreams of a dependent and demanding infant.

The early stages of a relationship, where bonds are weak and need nurturing, can also be symbolised in this way.

Pregnant women and new mothers report many dreams of babies, sometimes neglected or hurt, sometimes happy or even talkative, and these simply reflect the your deep feelings and fears or hopes regarding impending or new parenthood.

Basement

This lower, underground level of a dream house indicates the subconscious.

A cluttered basement or a dank one indicate issues you need to deal with.

A dark basement explored with a torch or lantern shows you are willing to face fears and your shadow to discover more of yourself.

Threatening evil creatures of one kind or another in the basement show strong fears of confronting unresolved parts of your psyche.

Bathroom

Besides the very obvious physiological aspect that dreaming of a bathroom or toilet may simply indicate that the bladder is full, and is thus the body trying to wake you, searching for a toilet and being unable to find one that is usable often symbolises fears of letting go emotionally.

If the search leads to filthy or blocked toilets, you may have emotions deeply repressed and fear that these hidden aspects of yourself are unclean.

Toilets without walls or doors can express fears you will 'expose' too much of yourself if you show your true feelings.

Dreams of defecation can indicate you feel the need to empty all your frustrations and anger out on someone.
Being smeared with another's faeces reflects the feeling that someone has soiled you with their dirty business.

Beach

Since the shore is where the realms of water and land meet, a dream set at the beach symbolises a time of transition, especially one where emotions are at the fore.

If you are standing on the earth, hesitating whether to enter the waves, you may have fears of admitting to certain emotions.

A dream of the beach can also indicate the meeting of issues from the subconscious and conscious minds, bringing with it a new awareness or acknowledgement of some aspect of personality previously denied.

Beast (monster, etc)

While it may seem obvious to identify a beast or monster with someone who is being aggressive or unpleasant to you in your waking life, it almost always represents some part of your deeper self—your animal nature or the unconscious and primal drives at work within you.

If the beast is chained or caged it indicates powerful repression at work in your waking life.

Confronting the monster or beast in the dream and be-friending it is indicative of the psyche's goal to embrace the whole self and integrate the primitive with the higher order consciousness.

Bees

Bees are a sign of activity and productivity but also refer to your social life.

They also tend to be a positive signifier of happiness and more specifically success in love.

In a business sense, like an industrious hive of activity,

bees point towards good earnings and profitable dealings.

Bird
(also see specific birds)

A symbol of nature and spirit, a bird may be the subconscious inviting you to enter a more spiritual realm.

Caged birds indicate hopes and dreams trapped and not free to fly.

A bird in flight represents achievement of your goals and possibly the attainment of happiness.

Dead birds represent unfulfilled or aborted dreams.

Bite/Bitten
Being bitten brings to a close emotions and fears about vulnerability from something threatening or unresolved. The trigger event is signified by what is doing the biting.

You biting someone, or something, indicates your preparedness to take on a venture or deal with a situation which may seem impossible to resolve or achieve and which you might normally be afraid of or uncertain about getting on with—literally, 'sinking your teeth' into something.

Blindness
Loss or lack of sight suggests an inability to see reality as it is, or a strong feeling of not knowing what is really going on.

The vulnerable feelings associated with lack of sight can also indicate a sense of being at the mercy of forces that won't show themselves.

If you dream that a friend or family member is blind, this may symbolise you feel they are ignorant of something important to your relationship with them and that they may need your help or guidance.

Sometimes, despite being blind in a dream, you can make surprising progress, representing the inner wisdom or intuition that guides you through circumstances where all the facts are not known.

Blood

Referring to the life force, a dream of blood spilt can symbolise the loss of the energy or resourcefulness necessary to achieve your goals.

It can also represent sacrifice.

Blood on your hands in a dream can indicate a feeling of guilt and a fear that others will see the 'crime' or failing that contributes to that feeling.

Body

A dead body can refer to some part of yourself that has been neglected to the point of atrophy and uselessness.

It may also indicate a relationship that has no life left in it.

Naked bodies can have connotations of sexuality or sensitivity, exposure or deliberate display.

Box

Traditionally a symbol of the vagina, a box can represent female sexuality.

If the box is damaged it can refer to harmful sexual memories, or to fears about being able to control and integrate sexuality.

In rare cases it can refer to reproductive health.

In quite a different interpretation, a box can also refer to feelings of being trapped, or 'boxed in' by circumstances or a relationship.

Just as with Pandora's Box which is a famous myth of troubles emerging through promises broken and warnings unheeded, a box that seems threatening or spills unpleasant contents might suggest fear of some impending trouble as a result of disobedience or curiosity.

Bridge

Traditionally, a bridge symbolises the passing from this life to the next, and recently deceased relatives may appear standing on a bridge.

Also a strong symbol of transition, of crossing from one stage of life to another, a bridge can refer to successfully spanning a gap or a difficult and dangerous aspect of your life.

If the bridge is damaged, and thus you cannot get across it, there are obstacles standing in the way of the transition.

A bridge over water indicates safe crossing of emotions, while a bridge over a ravine means you have managed to make it through a time when loss or gaps in your knowledge or experience could have been dangerous.

Burden

The carrying of a load in a dream indicates you feel weighed down by your problems, or you are carrying excessive responsibility.

It can also represent emotional baggage that needs to be dumped before you can move on to psychic health.

The nature of the burden can give clues to the source of the weight:

✦ If it consists of domestic items, perhaps family responsibilities are threatening to become too much

✦ If it is clothing, you may feel the need to assume personas to appear acceptable to others

✦ A burden of books can represent an overload of ideas

✦ If you are carrying another person, this symbolises that a relationship feels like a dead weight, although a dead body on your back is more likely to refer to an outdated or superseded aspect of yourself that you no longer need to carry about with you.

C

Car

Just as in life a car gets you from one place to the next, a dream car represents the journey of your life, although it can also represent your attitude towards your own body, the vehicle in which your soul travels.

An out of control car means you feel that things are overwhelming you with their speed and direction.

If you are driving your own car and the brakes don't work, this can symbolise you feel things are going too fast for you to feel comfortable and fear that something may bring you to a sudden and potentially harmful halt.

A car reversing may mean you feel that you are getting nowhere in life.

Being in the back seat of the car indicates you are not in control of your life and that someone else is making decisions for you and setting your life's direction. It is up to you decide, given your current life circumstances, whether this is a positive or negative thing.

The make and model of the car will have some significance too—note this carefully because as indicated earlier this tells you something significant about your feeling towards your body.

Candle

The candle can symbolise spiritual light and guiding wisdom, especially if you are carrying it or if another dream character uses it to guide you in the dark.

Phallic in shape, a candle can also represent male sexuality and your feelings about this according to the state it is in.

Note such things as whether it is lit or unlit, its size and its colour.

Cave

The classic interpretation of the cave is that it represents the womb—a dark, yet safe and nurturing place of secrets.

C

It can be also be a symbol of the unconscious, and if in your dream you meet an old man or woman in the cave, can indicate you are in touch with your inner wisdom.

Treasure in the cave can show you know your own worth in the deepest sense.

Chasm

A yawning gap that seems bottomless may indicate you are confronting fears of death or grief.

It can also represent the unconscious—the aspects of yourself beyond your control.

Child

A child can mean playfulness, creativity or reconnecting to some undeveloped part of yourself.

A malnourished or ill child can indicate you have neglected some need or that because of trauma, an aspect of your personality remains locked in childhood, not maturing.

If the child is demanding, this can symbolise it is important to address issues surrounding your inner child.

A healthy, happy child reflects a well-integrated inner child, and your ability to know when it is appropriate to play and indulge yourself.

Circle

A circle has no beginning and no end and as such indicates perfection or eternity.

A circle of people in a dream can represent harmony and the support that surrounds you.

If you are drawing circles or moving around in circles, this can symbolise you are completing projects or bringing relationships to their completion or fruition.

Your emotions on awakening are important and if feelings of frustration accompany this kind of dreaming, you can interpret it as acknowledgement of feeling trapped or in a rut of some kind.

City
A busy, crowded metropolis indicates you feel trapped and pressured in a situation not natural to you.

An empty city indicates you feel the odd one out in some area of your life.

Being lost in a city indicates anxiety about your current circumstances and the desire to find your way to a more comfortable scenario.

Being in an ancient city, or one clearly not of your time, indicates long standing social structures and values which may support you but which may also hold you back.

Closet
Being confined in a closet or cupboard or other dark enclosed space indicates feelings of limitation regarding your psyche.

Dreaming of hiding in such a space is a sign of you trying to avoid facing up to your own inadequacies.

C

Clothes

Just as nudity is covered by clothing in real life, dream clothing represents the personas you present to protect your vulnerability or conceal weakness.

The nature of the clothes can vary enormously but there are clues to interpretation:

✦ Beautiful garments can symbolise you feel successful in your interactions, while dirty or torn clothes suggest feelings of unworthiness, or of being judged.

✦ Oversized clothing can indicate feelings of needing to stretch yourself to gain acceptance, while tight, small clothing shows you have outgrown some habits or ways of relating.

Wearing clothes of the opposite sex might suggest you have confusion about how to present yourself along gender lines.

Coffin

A symbol of death in life, a coffin in your dreams can refer to anxieties about death, but can also refer to the end of a stage in your life.

If you recognise the person in the coffin, perhaps you feel that your relationship with them has died out.

Being in a coffin can indicate you feel trapped in a very small space and that your creativity and life force is being threatened, whereas rising from a coffin symbolises a new beginning.

Colours

As indicated earlier, colours all have specific meanings. Take special note of out of the ordinary colours (for example a pink cow) and overlay meanings accordingly.

+ Beige: everything related with this colour denotes neutrality and detachment and the possible absence of good communication

+ Black: signifies isolation and a transition period; it also shows up conflicts and friction with relations and friends

+ Blue: denotes a great source of inner peace and is a symbol of contentment

+ Brown: an auspicious colour to dream about, signifies freedom, success, money and happy and long-lasting unions

+ Grey: relates to a period of transition—if shiny it signifies peace, if dull, fear

+ Green: signifies growth and serenity and the chance of great pleasures from simple things

+ Orange: indicates passion in every aspect of your life

+ Pink: associates with tenderness and love

+ Purple: signifies great aspirations and understanding of the visible and invisible realms; also a symbol of creativity

+ Red: indicates great passion and sensitivity in your emotional relationships.

+ Turquoise: indicates new opportunities and the successful completion of projects

+ White: signifies people feel they can rely on you; it is also a symbol of an abundance of energy and vitality

✦ Yellow: indicates confidence in yourself and your abilities but also that there is the potential to encounter opposition.

Cow

Cows promise abundance, productivity and prosperity, gained from a consistent and almost docile approach to work.

They do, however, also indicate you should keep a close eye on your affairs, particularly in the professional realm.

Crossroads

When travelling, a crossroads demands the decision of which direction one needs to take, and thus in a dream it represents an issue or phase that requires a clear-cut choice, and possibly a ninety degree turn.

If there are clear signposts, this can suggest you feel you have all you need to make that decision. If there are no guides, perhaps you feel a bit lost and really don't know what to do.

D

Dagger

This can be a sexual symbol for men and can indicate a desire for physical relations, whereas for a female it indicates uncertainty or even fear about a relationship.

It can also refer to strong feelings of anger, and a desire to strike out at your circumstances.

As an instrument for cutting, if you wield it in the dream, this can indicate you have intellectual clarity and sharp insight that cuts to the core of the issue.

Dark

Darkness is a symbol of unconsciousness, or possibly ignorance.

The dark of night suggests a deep feeling that you lack the necessary knowledge about something in your life and feel vulnerable and uncertain as a result.

Prolonged or unnatural darkness suggests a situation in which you feel overwhelmed and unable to find any light of wisdom or knowledge.

Death

This is the symbol of change in most dreams as every ending in life is merely the herald of a new beginning.

If the dream is of someone deceased in your family or a friend, this can suggest the breakdown, major change or end of a relationship.

The death of a child can reflect a parent's anxieties about

the child, but should not be taken as a premonition.

If you dream of your own death, or believe yourself to be dead in a dream, this symbolises the end of old ways of relating and acting and transition to a new way of living.

Desert

The barrenness of a desert can symbolise feelings of being in an emotional wasteland.

If you are lost and thirsty in your dream, then the desert is an inhospitable place, and you need to find water –your emotional spring –in order to survive the crisis.

It can also indicate either your creativity is dried up or that you feel barren of ideas and resources.

Digging

Turning over soil and going deep into the earth can suggest you are getting in touch with buried aspects of yourself.

Alternately, it may indicate you are trying to get to the bottom of some puzzle or confusing aspect of your life, or searching the past for clues to the present.

Burying something suggests there is something you are trying to hide.

Doctor

A doctor appearing in your dreams is a symbol of the healing forces in your life, representing the healing of a problem that has incapacitated you.

If you are the doctor in the dream you may feel you are acting in a healing role in the lives of those around you.

A surgeon, especially where you find you are in the role, suggests you may need or want something cut from your life that is holding you back.

D

Door

The appearance of a door in your dreams changes in meaning, depending on whether the door is open or closed.

Just as an open door in life is an opportunity and an invitation, in your dream it suggests you are being beckoned to a new stage of life and there is no obstacle in your way.

A closed door can suggest you see there is some opportunity but you do not know how to make the most of it, possibly feeling thwarted and blocked.

Seriously ill people sometimes dream of a door, which can represent their feelings about impending death.

Dragon

A dragon can be interpreted as a symbol of power and sexual potency.

If it is destructive, it suggests these forces are out of control in your life whereas if it is approachable, it indicates you are comfortable with these aspects.

If you are dealing with an overwhelming and forceful individual in your life, that person can be represented by a dream dragon.

Good luck can also be indicated and sometimes the dragon represents spiritual power or the amassing of 'jewels of wisdom'.

E

Earthquake

The upheaval of an earthquake literally suggests something needs to be totally shaken up in your life.

Alternatively, it can reflect feelings you have of a potential impending cataclysm in some aspect of your life.

Electric shock

A dream of an electric shock may symbolise you have been touched by, or are in possible close contact with, a destructive force of some kind.

However, the force may be usable—if your feeling upon waking is not negative, electricity can symbolise a flooding through you of new creative energies and emotional forces that will animate you in new ways.

Elephant

Elephants are associated with the power of the mind, wisdom and intelligence.

They are also a sign of persistence against the odds.

Overall, they are a very positive element to a dream and can bring with them a sense of dignity and distinction.

Elevator

The status and location of your mental and spiritual awareness, related to the mind, are indicated by a dream of an elevator.

To dream of a slow elevator or one that stops and won't let you get to the floor you need is an indication of frustration and impatience to achieve something important.

If you get out at the wrong floor in your dream, this is a clear sign that even if you think you have reached the end point of some situation you still haven't truly found what you are seeking.

Engagement

A betrothal or engagement symbolises you have given your commitment to a project or relationship and, although your goal is not yet attainable, you are well on the way to achieving it.

It can also symbolise the impending union of previously contrasting forces in your life, or aspects of your own psyche.

Envelope

The dream envelope can symbolise a secret or some kind of subterfuge linked to emotions or events in your own or another's life.

Rarely do dreams of an envelope bearing bad news come

true—as with most dream symbols, they focus on aspects of your psyche or current circumstances and the emotions surrounding them.

Eruption

If feelings are being repressed, a dream of an eruption suggests things are about to burst out in a potentially destructive way. Emotions, if not properly channelled, will break forth and cause more harm than if the pressure had been let off gradually in a controlled way.

This symbol can also represent the imminence of new understanding or insight that will dramatically alter the landscape of your mind.

Escape

Successfully fleeing captors or something chasing you reflects a feeling of needing to outwit or outrun forces which could hold you back or harm you either in your personal or professional life.

If your escape is through trapdoors or secret exits, you have some tricks up your sleeve to get yourself out of trouble.

If someone helps you escape, the aid may be an aspect of yourself or actually another person.

Exam

These dreams often arise when you feel you are being judged or tested in some area of your life—perhaps you have set impossible standards for yourself, or someone else is expecting too much of you. There is a feeling of being called to account.

If you are ill-prepared for the exam, anxieties and lack of confidence surround the issue.

It is possible your dream is telling you that your decisions will be tested and you should have a thorough understanding of the reasons behind them before proceeding.

Excrement

Dreaming of excrement or defecation should not necessarily be taken literally!

If it is your own, although the obvious interpretation is that something unsightly and repulsive to others has come out of you—an idea or something you said—such can also suggest you have been creative and that things will grow and prosper in the fruits of your labour. Excrement is manure, after all.

If the excrement belongs to others, perhaps you feel like you are wallowing in other people's dirty business.

A further interpretation is that it may signify some aspect of your life is useless now, even if it has nourished you in the past, and that you have let go of it as it has become a burden.

F

Faceless

A faceless person is a common symbol of the unknown and usually reveals doubts about someone in your life—they are keeping their true nature hidden. If you wish to identify this individual, look for other clues/symbols in the dream.

It can also be a reminder to you that you never know another person completely and that to take someone for granted can be dangerous a thing.

Falling

To dream of falling is one of the more frequent dreams experienced by most of us.

A common interpretation is that you feel insecure and unsupported.

In some cases the dream can mean you have temporarily lost your grip on your values and feel you have let yourself down—you may be experiencing a drop in your confidence levels.

When interpreting this remember that in falling, you will eventually reach the ground and being grounded is not such a bad thing.

Most dreamers awaken before impact or discover at the last moment they can fly and so disaster is avoided—that they can overcome whatever it is that has caused you to fall.

Keep in mind that, had you not fallen in the first place you would never have made that discovery!

Father

Clearly, your feelings about your actual father will be the key to interpreting his appearance in your dreams.

If you feel positively about him, this dream figure represents strong family values or the aspects of your character and beliefs you have inherited from your father.

Negative emotions connected to your real father indicate some judgmental aspect of the dream father, with you feeling you were never good enough.

If your father disappointed you in some way, this figure can represent someone in authority in your life who is going to let you down.

Other interpretations of this symbol include the idea of procreation or creativity, a guide and protector, or even your own conscience.

If your father has recently died, these dreams may be the way for you to let him go and for him to bid you goodbye.

It may also represent an authority figure or supporter currently in your life who has a paternal influence on your life.

Fence

Like a wall, a fence is a barrier and can represent something in your life that stands between you and your goals.

Being enclosed by a fence suggests you feel trapped in some way.

Alternatively, in a positive sense, it can suggest you feel some sense of protection around you that keeps the wolves at bay.

If someone important to you is on the other side of the fence it could mean something has come between you, perhaps a social barrier or some unresolved issue.

Sitting on the fence is as literal as it sounds, indicating you need to make a decision and move to one side or the other.

Ferry

Traditionally the means of transport to the underworld or afterlife, a ferry can be a dream about an ending or an actual death you are grieving over.

If the ferry cannot land at some port, you may be wishing to move on from something (usually death or loss) but cannot.

On a more positive note, as ferries generally only travel in tranquil waters, it can also refer to your ability to let your emotions carry you safely to your destination.

Fire

Fire is traditionally a symbol of passion and sexual desire.

Thus, if the fire is out of control these forces are in danger of doing something destructive in your life, whereas a controlled fire, such as a fireplace, shows that the forces are contained and provide a positive influence.

Since a fire can purge and allow new growth it can also refer to some issue or person in your life that you need to totally rid yourself of so that you can start again.

If you are burned in the flame this may mean you feel a deep sense of suffering and pain or that a traumatic circumstance has purified you. You may also feel you are being sacrificed.

Flood

Overwhelming emotions are indicated in a dream of flooding.

If a dam bursts its banks, feelings held back for a long time are now breaking free.

Things carried away in a flood can represent what is at stake in this powerful outpouring.

If you manage to swim to safety, this shows you believe you can live through the moment of crisis.

If you must be rescued, you are relying on outside help and perhaps you do not want responsibility for the mopping up.

Flies

The appearance of a swarm of flies in your life indicates annoyance with friends or those close to you.

They also can be an indication that you are considering doing something reckless or foolish.

In their most negative sense, they can indicate the stalling of some success in your life until you can 'swat' away the obstacles to your success.

Flying

The very common dream of flying is a symbol of many things, among them your sense of personal power and ability to rise above circumstances.

In this case you may feel a great sense of freedom and achievement.

Personal spirituality can also be suggested as you rise to new heights and gain a different perspective.

The understanding of an important new concept in the

sphere of ideas can also be suggested.

If you take flight when something is chasing you, perhaps you are fleeing an issue or person and do not have the courage to turn and face them (again, look at other elements of your dream to determine what it is you are fleeing).

It can also suggest you resort to pie in the sky or fantasy when things get confrontational.

Forest

The forest, as a place of fertility and growth, can represent your natural creative urges—sexual, artistic or intellectual.

A dense dark forest indicates you have a strong sense of the power of these urges in your life.

A dream walk in the forest, just as in life, can be a restorative, health-giving experience.

Enjoying the growth and beauty of what is around you in the dream can indicate you are appreciating and enjoying the fruits of a project or relationship which has required an enormous amount of energy.

Fountain

A dream fountain is generally a healthy symbol of renewing life force, suggesting cleansing, thirst being quenched and peace. The water of emotion is channelled and used for a positive purpose.

A sexual meaning can also apply. Ejaculation is suggested

by the fountain and if the figure of someone you desire is also in the dream, it makes this a probable interpretation.

Frozen

Ice, snow, blizzards or extreme cold in a dream can all suggest you are in an emotionally deprived relationship or work situation where you have been frozen out of the decision-making process. Perhaps you yourself feel frozen, unable to commit or to let yourself feel your true emotions.

Gambling

A dream of gambling can symbolise a need in you to leave what is safe and sure and take a few risks.

If the gambling pays dividends, your spirit may be telling you it will be worth it to let loose and see what life brings for a while.

Losses through gambling in a dream may indicate some project you are undertaking is risky and the outcome far from assured.

Such dreams should not be taken as precognitive or as assurances that if you take a lottery ticket this week you will win!

Garbage

Refuse and things cast aside as useless in a dream usually indicate outdated ideas, opinions or attitudes that will be of no further benefit to you—a symbol of spring-cleaning your mind or heart.

Being overwhelmed by garbage can suggest you are feeling that nothing much useful is coming your way in relationships or work, just discards and junk.

Garden

A garden in a dream can reveal what you are doing with your innate abilities. Are you feeding and watering them so they blossom, or have you neglected them so that they wither and die?

A flower-filled garden, complete with birds and sunshine, suggests you are growing something beautiful in your life.

It can also possibly refer to a pregnancy, or a relationship that is blooming.

An overgrown garden can suggest some aspects of your creativity are not being cultivated.

Ghost

Vestiges of the past are symbolised by a dream of a ghost. Something that used to be alive and powerful is no longer so—it may refer to the loss of memory or the loss of the power of your memories to shape the future.

If the ghost is someone you know, the influence of that person in your life is waning.

When accompanied by a feeling of dread, this can suggest there is something from the past that is threatening you now, perhaps an action that is coming back to haunt you.

Giraffe

A giraffe suggest that something is beyond your grasp or understanding.

Running away from a giraffe could be an indication of loss or defeat because of your inability to cope or manage a situation.

A giraffe coming at you without any threat can be seen as you recognising a challenge that can overwhelm you but which you know you must face up to.

A giraffe charging at you means you are beginning to panic because you are not adequately prepared for a situation.

Glass

Because glass is fragile, but can be deceptive as if it isn't really there, it often represents something you are barely aware of which forms an obstruction, such as social barriers, pride or ignorance.

If the glass forms a window through which you can see, it suggests opportunity, but there is still the need to break through the barrier to make the most of that chance.

A looking glass can suggest self-analysis or self-absorption.

Frosted or dirty glass means there is something obscuring your vision, while wearing glasses shows that the means is available to you to see things clearly.

Shattered glass can be a symbol of broken dreams.

Glove

Wearing gloves in a dream can suggest you are out of touch with what is going on.

Alternately it sometimes means you may wish to not have to handle something that is problematic or unpleasant.

Another interpretation is that you feel that you have to handle something with extreme care at the moment.

Goat

The goat is an ancient symbol of male fertility. It can refer to your own potency or latent energies or to the presence in your life of a male who desires or threatens you.

Goats in ancient times were sacrificed to the gods and so this may also represent aspects of yourself that you have had to 'kill' in order to achieve your goals.

If the goat in your dream is a nanny goat it can have a meaning similar to the fool. You may be experiencing annoyance at someone who is acting the goat, or getting on your goat.

Gold

A clear symbol of wealth, gold in a dream suggests spiritual richness.

If the gold is discovered with another person, it can suggest value in a relationship.

If it is offered to you, someone in your life has a valuable contribution to make.

Knowledge can also be represented by gold, as can a new and helpful insight.

Grandparents

Generally, seeing your grandparents in your dreams is symbolic of unconditional love and acceptance and may indicate you have within the ability to provide this—for yourself and others.

These symbols may also suggest inner wisdom that has stood the test of time—old-fashioned values that are worth keeping hold of.

If the grandparent is crippled or incapacitated perhaps in your life some source of moral strength is being threatened and needs attention.

Gun

A dream of bearing and using a gun can symbolise built-up frustrations and anger needing to be discharged in a controlled and non-harmful way.

A sexual interpretation is also possible if desires are being thwarted, but the warning is that these urges have the potential to do great harm.

Yet a further reading of this symbol may be that you feel you cannot face the world without a weapon of some kind, and that you approach life with the view that if you don't conquer it, it might conquer you.

In all cases it suggests some form of aggression.

H

Hair

A widely experienced symbol in dreams, the colour, condition, amount and placement of the hair all affect its interpretation:

+ Hair on the head tends to relate to mental faculties.

+ Brushing and styling hair can suggest mental activity or attention to thought processes and ideas.

+ Changing hair colour or style in a dream can indicate you are trying out new ways of thinking, new attitudes or beliefs.

+ Dishevelled or untidy hair can indicate your thoughts are confused.

+ Baldness can symbolise you are all out of ideas.

+ A shaved head can represent remorse or grief, or renunciation of some desire.

+ Genital or armpit hair represents sexuality and concealed sexual desires.

+ Facial hair on a woman in a dream can suggest the masculine side is trying to assert itself, as can chest hair.

Hand

Significant dream hands can be interpreted in a number of ways.

They can be symbols of nurturance or greed, of giving, hurting or grasping.

Gnarled, arthritic hands can suggest an inflexible approach to life, while injured hands can reveal a feeling of weakness in interacting with the world.

Hands adorned with rings can suggest power or wisdom—if these hands bless you in the dream, you may feel as if some gift has been bestowed by someone you admire.

Handbag

Generally the handbag is a symbol of female sexuality, specifically the uterus.

If it is damaged or things fall out of it, this can reflect feelings surrounding the inability to conceive.

A stolen handbag can indicate that fear and confusion surround sexuality.

The size and shape are important in interpreting this symbol—a large, ostentatious handbag might suggest you flaunt your feminine sexuality, while a coin purse can suggest the opposite.

Heaven

If you consider your waking life to be a 'hell', a dream of heaven is a compensatory dream, reminding you that such places do exist within yourself and that you can find them.

If you are a religious or spiritual person, dreaming of the celestial sphere can indicate you have found a moment of spiritual union or clarity or enlightenment.

If you are in love, this is about the happiness you know and believe to be eternal.

Hotel

Just as hotels are places of transient socialising in waking life, a dream of a hotel can indicate impermanence in a relationship.

It can also suggest you have a full social life, but many of the interactions are not of a lasting nature.

If you have lost your hotel key in the dream you may be feeling locked out of social opportunities and are seeking more from friendships.

Hiding

As you might expect, hiding can symbolise you are shying away from responsibility or from facing up to something which demands your attention. Perhaps you are covering something up and fear exposure?

Hiding an object suggests there is anxiety or guilt over some past actions.

Hill

Walking or climbing up a hill usually suggests a minor challenge in your life.

The hill may appear small in the dream, but as you go to climb it there is an ever-receding crest you struggle to attain. This can be interpreted as ongoing frustration in your personal or business life.

The hill may also represent some goal that requires effort.

Watching someone disappear over a hill can indicate there is a person in your life who is succumbing to age, or who you believe is past contributing anything.

Homosexuality

Psychological studies have shown we all potentially have elements of homosexuality in our psyche.

To dream of engaging in a homosexual act usually indicates not so much something to do with sexual orientation, but rather how strongly you feel engaged with your anima or animus.

It can, however, also indicate a need to develop that side of your nature.

If your dream lover of the same sex is significantly older, this may suggest a craving for maternal or paternal love.

House

In most dreams the house represents the self, and usually the body, although it can be a symbol of your psyche, the place where your thoughts and feelings dwell.

Damage to the house can suggest ill physical or mental health, while a rambling house with many rooms and gardens suggests a broad attitude to life that accommodates many different perspectives and encourages creativity.

A house with an open door suggests a welcoming personality, or alternatively can link to sexual promiscuity.

The various rooms of the house can suggest different aspects of your life:

+ the kitchen is associated with nourishment
+ the laundry with preparation of a persona
+ the bathroom with purification and cleansing
+ the bedroom hints at sexuality
+ a library can represent the importance of ideas and knowledge to you
+ an attic might refer to spiritual striving.

I

Illness

Sometimes precognitive but not usually, dreams of illness more often refer to things in your life not being well on an emotional or spiritual level.

Illness may also indicate something needs healing in your life, feelings attended to and disturbed memories laid to rest.

It is interesting to note that physically ill people will often dream of divorce or marriage breakdown as symbols of their illness.

Infidelity

If you dream your partner is being unfaithful this may be because you already have your suspicions. In such cases, the dreams can often confirm this.

However, another interpretation is that you feel you have been betrayed by family, friends or colleagues.

It can also suggest you have betrayed your own ideals and that your psychic unity is in danger of falling unless you bring the erring part of yourself back into the fold.

Insects

A plague of insects in a dream can be interpreted as meaning there are a host of small annoyances in your life— that many things are bugging you.

If they are ticks, this suggests these problems have potential to burrow deep into your life, while flies can indicate that too many ideas are buzzing around in your head.

A cricket singing in the darkness might mean your conscience is calling to you, reminding you of the right thing to do in times of temptation or despair.

Intruder

The stranger who breaks into your dream house can represent many things—perhaps you are feeling vulnerable and insecure, physically or mentally.

The intruder symbol can have sexual overtones—in a relationship you may feel invaded by your partner's demands.

Many dreams of intruders are semi-lucid in that you dream of being asleep in bed and waking to an intruder. This seems to be just a semi-conscious response to the physical paralysis of REM sleep.

Inarticulate

Being inarticulate or dumb in a dream can indicate you feel you have no voice or are not being listened to.

Anxieties about speaking up, and the consequences, may play out in such a dream.

Talking nonsense might suggest you have not clarified what you really think or believe and the dream is suggesting you pay attention to this.

Invisibility

Being invisible can indicate you are happily working behind the scenes, or you are frustrated because your contribution and needs are not being acknowledged. It is as if you don't exist.

Discovering you can become invisible to escape pursuers may suggest duplicity.

If something you are seeking becomes invisible this suggests you do not understand its true nature and that it will elude you until you discover it.

Ironing

A dream of ironing suggests you are straightening things out in your life, healing wounds and getting yourself ready to face the world again.

The iron itself can be a symbol of strong will and determination.

Island

An island is surrounded by water, cut off from the mainland, and thus an interpretation of this is that one part of your life has been carried away by emotions and cut adrift from the rest.

It can also refer to a feeling of being different or isolated from everyone else.

A tropical island can suggest you believe your isolation is

not only bearable but a boon.

A barren island suggests exile and loss, exclusion from society or family.

J

Jail

A dream of being imprisoned can be interpreted as you feeling caught or unfairly restrained in some area of your life.

It may alternatively suggest your creativity is being squashed and that you have no sense of freedom when it comes to expressing yourself. You may feel judged and condemned, but have no recourse to appeal.

Jewellery

As adornment, jewellery in a dream suggests superficial aspects of your nature.

It may indicate a desire to impress others and to dress up your real personality just for their benefit.

A crown or tiara can indicate you have attained a higher level of spirituality or that your intellect is vital and impressive.

A different interpretation is that it represents the gifts of love given you by family and friends.

Journey

The journey is a symbol of the whole of life and all the stages along the way.

Dreaming about packing and planning for a journey

suggests a new stage of life is opening up and soon you will find yourself in unfamiliar territory with many discoveries to make.

Leaving luggage behind may indicate you feel unprepared, but in fact it will enable to you travel more freely. What you left behind may be outdated and useless in this new place.

Different kinds of journeys suggest different things:

- ✦ a sea journey can suggest a great emotional component to a new beginning
- ✦ air flights suggest a fast paced transition
- ✦ journeys on foot, perhaps accompanied by others, are reminiscent of pilgrimages of old, and can be interpreted to mean you are on a spiritual quest and will discover many guides along the way.

Obstacles are inevitable on any journey and your overcoming them will provide you with traveller's tales when you reach your goal. Dream obstacles may be broken bridges, lack of signposts, steep hills or mountains, bad weather, vehicle breakdown, robbery or attack.

Enjoy your journey dreams—they will give you good guidance.

Juggling

A dream of juggling suggests you have many projects on the go at once and have to have all your wits about you to keep them from falling in a heap.

Perhaps you don't know which is the really important task or relationship to give priority to.

Jury

Sitting on a dream jury can symbolise your need to make a judgement on something in your work or personal life. You are not alone however—advice is available from others and you need to confer with them.

It can also be a symbol of your conscience questioning something you have done or said, or can reflect low self-esteem.

K

Key

A dream of a key can sometimes suggest you feel a solution to a problem is close at hand. It is perhaps an idea or a new understanding that will open up possibilities in the future.

If someone gives you a key, you may be about to receive guidance, but if you lose a key this suggests you do not make good use of the knowledge you have received.

Being a key-bearer can indicate you have been given new responsibilities.

Killing

The act of killing another in a dream usually hints at repressed anger, with the dream being a form of compensation or wish fulfilment.

The killing of an animal can indicate harsh repression of

basic instincts or drives

It can also mean you are prepared to sacrifice much to attain your goals.

King

A King figure generally refers to your feelings about your father and the power he holds in your life.

It can also symbolise the ruling presence of another male in your life, perhaps even your own masculine qualities of leadership, justice and action.

Kiss

A dream kiss can symbolise a coming together of opposites in your life.

It may suggest that a union of these opposites will grow into something stronger.

If you dream that someone you secretly desire kisses you, or allows you to kiss them, this is usually the acting out of repressed wishes and has no deeper significance.

A kiss can, however, can mean betrayal (as in Judas's kiss) and thus the feelings you have after this kind of dream are important.

Knapsack

A symbol of what you carry upon a journey, the knapsack in a dream can refer to all the memories, beliefs, values and attitudes you take with you through life.

If in the dream you sort through the knapsack and discard some objects that are unnecessary or too heavy, this suggests a spiritual stock-take and a lightening of your load as you throw away what you no longer need.

If your knapsack is stolen, it may seem in the dream that you cannot continue on your journey. This may be warning you that all you hold dear is under threat or simply that you must be prepared to protect what is basic to your sense of self.

Knitting

Knitting in a dream suggests some aspect of your life needs a lot of careful attention.

Knitting can also suggest you feel responsible for pulling together many strands in your life and dare not take a break in case something goes wrong.

If the knitting is knotted there are problems in something major in your life and a dropped stitch can indicate your fear that everything is about to unravel.

L

Labyrinth

A dream in which you must find your way through a labyrinth that you sense leads to something unknown at the centre indicates you are facing challenges which confuse you. Sometimes you feel that you are making no progress and are back where you started.

If a thread or trail of some kind guides you, this suggests you have access to spiritual wisdom and will find your way through and out.

Ladder

Climbing a ladder in a dream suggests you are striving for something out of reach.

Broken or slippery rungs might indicate the task is a dangerous one.

It may be interpreted also as reaching for spiritual wisdom and union.

If you reach the top of the ladder and can go no further, you may be unsure of what next steps to take to reach your goal.

Lake

A contained body of water suggests emotions controlled and tranquil.

However, in a less positive sense, it may also refer to stagnation.

A lake of clear reflections can symbolise clarity achieved through control, but dead trees or fish in the water can indicate that the water or emotions are poisoned and need to be flushed out.

Lameness

Injury or paralysis in a leg can symbolise your inability to make a move in a situation or relationship.

If you are lame in the right leg, the weakness may be linked to some aspect of masculine strength, whereas the left leg suggests the feminine side is being thwarted.

Whatever the cause, lameness represents stagnation and loss of opportunity.

Using a crutch to overcome the lameness indicates you are prepared to seek help to move forward.

Lantern

Just as a light shining in the night represents hope and safety, so too does a lantern in the dream darkness. As light of any kind symbolises spiritual wisdom and knowledge, a hand-held light suggests wisdom carefully tended.

If the light goes out you may be concerned that the knowledge or wisdom you have will not be enough to carry you through.

Leak

Water leaking in a dream suggests emotions which are not contained. If the leak is causing damage there is a negative outcome from these uncontrolled feelings.

As water is necessary for life, it can also symbolise energy—if leaking, something is draining away and it will be difficult for you to achieve your goals unless the leak is sealed.

The breaking of confidence, as in the leaking of information, is another interpretation of this symbol.

Lemon

Feelings of bitterness are suggested by a lemon—perhaps you have a sour taste in your mouth as the result of some problem at work or at home.

However, some cultures view lemons as health-giving and purifying, so the eating of a lemon in a dream may also be a positive sign.

If someone gives you a lemon, perhaps you are feeling that problems have been dropped in your lap.

Lightning

As such might suggest, lightning in a dream can indicate a sudden flash of insight or enlightenment, but equally it can indicate the sudden and explosive outlet of emotion, especially anger.

As an ironic play on the word, the dream may be telling you that you need to do some 'lightening up' in life and to not take things so seriously.

Revenge is another interpretation of this symbol, and if you are struck by lightning in the dream, this could be the meaning.

Lily

In Western culture, the Lily symbolises virginity and purity and the female aspect of God.

It is sometimes also associated with death but can also be the equivalent of the Indian culture's lotus flower as a symbol of enlightenment and harmony.

Lion

As a regal beast, the lion is a symbol of kingship and authority. It may be a disguised image of your father, but equally may represent fierce love.

A lion attacking you suggests you may fear the powerful

aspects of your father, or your own masculinity.

Locker

A locker is where you keep your valuables and so in a dream may symbolise your sense of identity.

If you dream of a school locker as an adult, the anxieties you are experiencing about your identity may be similar to those of adolescence.

A locker that will not lock can reflect feelings of vulnerability.

Log

Carrying a log or stubbing your toe on one in a dream can indicate you are burdened by dead wood at work or in your relationship. This may be a person but is more likely to be attitudes or practices that serve no current purpose.

A burning log can refer to male sexuality.

A log may be a pun for record keeping and if this is what you stub your toe on, the dream may be telling you that you need to keep better records in future.

Lungs

Lungs featuring in a dream can be a symbol of your ability to take and give in life.

Healthy lungs can suggest you have a good balance of these two aspects of life but breathing difficulties can refer to feeling pressure from without that is stopping you experiencing life to the fullest.

M

Machine

A dream machine may refer to the mechanical aspects of your life—the things you do automatically and without much thought.

If it breaks down perhaps there has been an interruption to your routine

A machine can also be interpreted as meaning the automatic functions of the body, for example the pumping of your heart, and so may be a health-focussed dream.

A person in your dream who is part human and part machine can suggest you view someone as an un-thinking robot with no flexibility or creativity. They are however reliable and predictable.

Magician

A dream of a magician or trickster can mean you or another is cleverly confusing and deceiving others.

It can also be interpreted as an attempt by your conscious mind to manipulate the forces deeper in your psyche. Such efforts may appear to work but they are illusory only.

Make-up

Dreaming of make-up usually refers to the persona or face you wear in public.

As the focus of a dream it can reflect anxieties about appearance—a sense that without clever concealment and enhancement the true face cannot be revealed.

If the make-up is smudged perhaps you feel that your mask is inadequate and does not convince others.

Market

A busy marketplace can symbolise the give and take of life, the commerce or trafficking in experience and feelings, love and hate, desire and generosity and everything in between.

Having no money to spend can suggest feelings of inadequacy or of having nothing to offer the world.

An important meeting in the marketplace can indicate that all the interactions of your life are leading you to union with your higher self.

M

Marsh

A bog, swamp or marsh in a dream can indicate you feel bogged down by circumstances, unable to move ahead, fearing that either drowning or slow burial under emotional sludge is a possibility.

Medicine

Taking or giving medicine in a dream suggests having to swallow a bitter pill in order to regain mental or emotional health.

Merry-go-round

A roundabout or merry-go-round can be a symbol of playfulness and childlike joy, but equally it can be like the roundabout upon the road—a symbol of getting nowhere.

Some aspect of work or relationship may be repeating itself over and over so that you feel you are stuck on a merry-go-round.

The circle of the merry-go-round can be a positive thing, suggesting completion of a cycle.

Mice

Rodents or mice foretell some kind of domestic trouble that requires your attention.

They can also indicate business affairs may take a negative turn until you can rid yourself of certain annoyances.

Mine

This symbol refers to the depths of the subconscious and unconscious.

Descending into a mine in a dream indicates you are entering a dark realm beneath the surface of your daily life. If you have a torch and come back to the top with valuable items in your hand, the descent has been successful and your psyche will be healthier as a result.

Money

Dreams of finding money are rarely prophetic. Rather, this is a symbol of discovering inner wealth, or blessing in your relationships and other situations.

Money in a dream can represent energy or the forces

that rule your world.

Having insufficient money can reflect anxieties about your worth or self-esteem.

Monkey
In Eastern culture the monkey was a god, representing the combination of instinctual and intellectual energies. Cunning, cleverness, playfulness and unpredictability are his qualities.

If you dream a monkey is teasing you, perhaps your dream is calling you to let go of some of the discipline in your life and let loose for a while.

A less positive interpretation is that you feel someone is making a monkey out of you.

Nail
A nail is a small thing but it holds big things together and as such can represent some important detail that needs attention in a problem you are working on.

If in the dream you are dropping nails and finding it hard to hammer them in, this can suggest you need to pay more attention to small details and follow them through if you do not want things to fall apart.

Naked
Being naked, an extremely common dream, generally suggests feeling of exposure and vulnerability.

The setting of your nakedness in the dream reflects the cause of your anxiety. If at work perhaps you feel unprepared and fear being 'seen through' by your colleagues. If naked in the street perhaps you feel vulnerable in social situations.

If this nakedness is unnoticed by others in the dream it could be that you are oversensitive and worry too much about how others might judge you.

Another interpretation is possible however— your nudity can suggest you may wish to reveal your true feelings to others.

If you are naked and comfortable with a lover, this can suggest a harmony in your psyche, or honesty in your relationships.

Neck

The neck is an extremely vulnerable part of the body and represents many things in a dream. The back of the neck can suggest vulnerability, while the throat can refer to issues of feeling unable to breathe or to express your own voice.

A dream that focuses on the neck can suggest caution, pride or boldness, depending on your attitude. Perhaps you are sticking your neck out or revealing your vulnerability. If positive feelings surround the dream, then it can suggest achievement and success, as you 'hold your head up'.

Another interpretation is that you feel up to your neck in problems and fear that you will soon drown.

Necktie

The interpretation of this symbol depends on other aspects of your life.

If wearing a tie is not something you usually do, then to dream of one suggests you are in an uncomfortable situation.

Given that in a professional environment the necktie is a mark of acceptability and respectability, this may be an alternative meaning.

However, a tie can also be a symbol of something holding the head to the body, thus indicating your ideas are in danger of taking off into unreal realms and that you need to be more grounded.

If the necktie is too tight, issues of voicelessness or feeling choked by circumstances are hinted at.

Needle

Sewing in a dream can be a symbol of stitching together various parts of your life, to make something new.

A needle dropped and searched for can indicate you are frustrated by small details which are stopping you from pulling everything together.

Using a needle to repair a garment in a dream can indicate you are using your insight and mental sharpness to fix problems in your life.

As a sharp implement, a needle can refer to the male sex organ—in medieval times, sewing was a euphemism for the sex act.

Neighbour

Neighbours, in your waking life, can be a nuisance or a support and in a dream both meanings are possible.

The neighbour lives closest to your house and so is understood to represent your conscious personality in a dream.

If there is harmony between you and your neighbour in the dream, this suggests your inner and outer selves co-exist happily.

If there is tension or argument, then a rift may have occurred in your psyche that needs healing.

Nest

A nest is traditionally interpreted as the female sex organ.

In a dream it may refer to sexuality or to anxieties about conception.

It can also be a symbol of home and security, comfort and nurturing.

An empty nest in a dream may refer to fears about children leaving the maternal influence or family vulnerability.

Night

The most common meaning of this symbol is ignorance, obscurity and lack of vision.

Night is the home of fears and being without the light of knowledge may cause these to arise. The dream may be portraying how you feel about some aspect of your life—literally, 'in the dark'.

Noose

The noose, as a symbol of death, can represent a fear of dying physically, or emotionally being left to hang.

Because it surrounds the throat it can also be interpreted

as indicating a sense of choking or being stifled in a relationship or other circumstance.

Nose
Dreaming of a prominent nose, either on your face or on another dream-figure can represent curiosity or an unhealthy interest in the affairs of others.

Are you sticking your nose into someone else's business or they into yours?

As the nose is also the sense organ of smell, this can also indicate you can 'smell a rat' or that there is something fishy going on.

Numbers
The numbers 1-9 can have mystical symbolism, but your own life circumstances can also contribute to the meaning. The number of children you have, your birth date and a lucky number are all influences on interpreting the occurrence of a number in a dream.

A study of numerology will reveal the full meanings of numbers, but there may also be relevance to the chakras of yogic practice. Each of the seven chakras is associated with health and spiritual issues and it is an interesting study to seek this meaning in your dream.

1—the number of wholeness and completeness. It can suggest independence and strength or leadership.

2—represents the coming together of opposites.

3—a triangle or trinity. It suggests balance.

4—stability and being grounded.

5—the senses or practical issues that require a

hands-on approach.

6—the number of love.

7—traditionally powerful; gives access to secret knowledge.

8—infinity.

9—completion or the end of a cycle, as in gestation.

Numbers can also suggest that the seconds are running out on a pressing issue and that you need to make a decision because the number of opportunities is not unlimited.

O

Oak

The tall oak tree is usually associated with strength, endurance and knowledge.

Oak tree roots go deep—if you dream of sheltering under or climbing an oak such is a sign of accessing ancient wisdom.

It can also reflect good health and is a symbol of life.

A tree with a broken branch may suggest health issues in the body or even family disruption or loss.

Ocean

Classically, the ocean is symbolic of emotions where storms can arise without warning and lives are threatened by enormous forces.

If the ocean in your dream is wild, and you are trying to stay afloat, it suggests your emotional life is troubled. Even if you are not conscious of this, the dream would indicate that deep down there are some very strong feelings at work.

A tsunami or tidal wave might be your spirit telling you that if issues are not addressed some destructive emotions are going to overwhelm you.

A calm sea can reflect that all is well in your relationships and with your inner life.

Fishing in the sea indicates a plumbing of your emotional depths to draw up new insights and understanding.

Finding sunken treasure or life forms can suggest that deep within your psyche are undiscovered strengths and beauty.

Octopus

A dream of an octopus is usually frightening because, as creatures of the deep, they represent unknown parts of the psyche.

If you are attacked by a large octopus perhaps feelings of being sucked dry by strong forces or of being outnumbered in strategies is the issue.

An octopus can also suggest greed.

If the number eight is significant to you this is another factor in interpretation.

Office

To dream of an office, the extreme opposite of the social sphere, suggests connecting to the control centre or administrative aspects of your psyche—your values and beliefs.

A disorganised office can suggest you are losing control of issues in your life through not maintaining strong values and a belief system.

Alternatively, the office can literally represent your working life and the challenges you face there.

If there is something in your office that should not be there, consider what it is and the meaning implicit to it as the possible solution to an issue involving this aspect of your life.

Oil

Oil can be a symbol of slipperiness and cunning—of getting out of difficult situations in a less than positive way.

Conversely, it can point to peacemaking abilities and oiling the machinery of a situation to bring about a positive conclusion.

Onion

An onion is a many-layered vegetable and as such can represent a problem that has many aspects and is difficult to solve, with each layer revealing yet another set of problems.

If someone gives you an onion in the dream, this can often be the meaning.

Cutting up onions, suggestive of cooking or providing

nourishment for your family or yourself, can be a sign of needing comfort of this kind or wanting to provide it.

However, it can also indicate that tears are not far away.

In ancient times, onions were considered integral to spiritual and physical health and were believed to ward off evil, so an onion in the house in your dream suggests you are successfully warding off illness or psychic attack.

Orgy

Scenes of excessive sexual indulgence and orgiastic activity are usually interpreted as dreams of unfulfilled desires.

Orgies do not suggest you lack control—rather, they are an acknowledgement that inside all of us exist primitive urges. This is the psyche compensating for the discipline of our waking moments.

Oven

An oven is often seen to represent the womb, or the nurturing centre of your life.

An oven that will not heat can suggest difficulties with pregnancy, or a cold emotional environment.

As a crucible of transformation, the oven is also a symbol of change.

Something cooking in the oven may suggest a project or idea that is growing and developing.

A kitchen with no oven can refer to family life lacking in maternal guidance or warmth.

P

Packing

A dream of packing up a house or packing for a holiday can indicate a new phase of your life is beginning. You may be sorting out what from your old life is going to fit into the new.

Trying to pack inappropriate things such as hot food or pets can suggest there are domestic issues you wish to stow away and not address.

Packing and then leaving the boxes behind can represent a desire to run away from the challenges in your life and to avoid responsibility. However, it can also suggest that there are attitudes you can leave behind which are no longer appropriate.

Palace

Just as a dream house is your body or self, a palace can symbolise your cultural heritage or intellect.

The storehouse of your knowledge, it is a grand and wonderful place.

Living in a dream palace can reflect appreciation of the wealth of your family and cultural background, but may also indicate a fantasy.

'Castles in the sky' can compensate for daily drudgery,

so this may also be the meaning of such a dream.

Parachute

A safety measure, a parachute can symbolise you are flying high in emotions or endeavours and, although you have a fear of falling, a means of a soft landing is available to you.

If in the dream the parachute fails to open, this could indicate some help being offered will not materialise, or that a plan you have will let you down.

Paralysis

In REM sleep the body experiences a mild paralysis and thus a semi-lucid dream where you are unable to move or are trying to wake up can simply reflect this physiological state.

However, a dream where you are unable to get where you want to go can suggest you feel powerless in your current circumstances and are making no progress.

Alternatively, the interpretation may be that you are avoiding responsibility or do not wish to be involved in something.

If your partner or someone important to you is beckoning you and you cannot move in that direction perhaps there are difficulties in the relationship and you are resisting making the first move.

Paralysis in a dream caused by terror may be a symbol that some deep fear is stopping you from moving on.

Parcel

Dreaming about a parcel may symbolise a latent talent that you have not developed or explored.

It can sometimes be a symbol of unopened memories, perhaps repressed trauma.

Another interpretation is that a new phase of your life is about to open.

Sinister parcels are sometimes interpreted to mean unacknowledged passions such as hate or anger.

Passport

A passport is commonly interpreted to mean your sense of identity.

It may also symbolise your sense of belonging in your family or community.

Losing your passport in a dream may suggest that your self-esteem and self-identity are vulnerable. This is especially relevant if in the dream you have been staying in a foreign country and wish to leave.

The passport may also symbolise the means by which you will pass from one phase of your life to the next, as it is associated with a journey.

The photo in the passport, if it is not of you, may suggest the personality growth required to move on.

Path

As you might expect, seeing a path in your dreams most commonly represents your chosen life course.

A wide clear path can suggest you feel comfortable about

your direction and know how to get there.

An overgrown neglected path may indicate you feel uncertain about the immediate future and are questioning past choices.

A path cluttered with obstacles can indicate challenges or obstacles in the way of you getting where you want to go.

Pay

Handing over money for goods or services can symbolise the cost of a relationship or professional endeavour.

If you have insufficient money it may suggest you are unable or unwilling to pay the price and that you need to reconsider what you truly must give up to resolve this situation.

Peacock

A dream of a peacock suggests pride and ostentation.

This could come in the form of you possibly being affected by someone who is a show off—or that you are caught up in showing off yourself.

Eastern cultures sometimes see the peacock as a symbol of new beginnings because it loses its beauty then grows it back, so this may also be a symbol of new beginnings.

Pearl

A pearl develops in a secret place deep in the ocean and as such it can symbolise spiritual wisdom in a dream.

It may also suggest you have inner riches of which you are as yet unaware.

Yet another interpretation is of hard-won knowledge and wisdom, grown out of pain and discomfort.

Sometimes, the pearl can be a symbol of pregnancy.

A broken string of pearls can indicate advice that is not heeded.

Pedestal

The saying 'to put someone on a pedestal' is the guide to interpreting this symbol in many dreams.

If in the dream you are on the pedestal, perhaps others are holding you in high regard.

Someone else on the pedestal may indicate you worship this person or aspects of their personality.

An unsteady pedestal suggests this lofty position may only be temporary.

Penis

In men's dreams the penis symbolises potency and sexual identity.

The state of the penis can reflect how they feel about this aspect of their lives.

It may refer to actual sexual activity or your sense of power and ability to impact upon the world.

It can also refer to creativity.

If a women dreams of a penis, such can suggest desire for sexual union or a need for more masculine qualities in her life.

A woman with a dream penis can be interpreted as a strong sense of power or may indicate a compensatory wish for potency.

Perspiration

To dream of excessive sweating can indicate strong anxieties, fear or even guilt.

If in the dream others notice and respond negatively to your perspiration this may mean you fear that your feelings are leaking out of you and causing problems.

However, it may also suggest that purification is at work in you and some unpleasant influences are being cleansed.

P

Photograph

The usual interpretation of dreaming of a photograph is that it indicates a memory.

The subject of the photograph will guide you to the real memory.

However, lost or damaged photographs in a dream can reflect anxieties about the past or, equally, about a failing memory.

If in the dream you take a film to be developed into photographs it can mean you are bringing to the surface buried memories or forgotten incidents from the past.

Piano

As a dream symbol the piano can mean self-expression.

A focus upon the keyboard, however, may refer to seeing things too black and white, or may even symbolise the number eight, which can mean infinity.

If the piano is silent, the meaning may be that self-expression is stifled or that some enjoyment has been cut off in your life.

An out of tune piano can symbolise disharmony in a relationship or within yourself.

Pig

The obvious associations of a dream containing a pig are gluttony and being unclean, but it may also symbolise intelligence.

Stubbornness and determination can also be represented in the figure of a pig.

A dream of a sow might suggest fertility and nurturing qualities or a need or desire for the same.

Pimple

Dreams involving facial blemishes, such as pimples, can symbolise concerns we have about how we present ourselves to others.

Is our persona marred by a blemish?

Fretting about the pimple with no-one else noticing can indicate you are focussing on something minor and unimportant and your fears are ungrounded.

Also in a literal sense such a dream may simply reflect real concerns you have about your appearance.

Pirate

A dream pirate can suggest you feel that someone is plundering from you and not giving anything back.

Lawlessness and greed are also implicated in this figure.

Outlawed emotions can be suggested, especially if the sea upon which the pirate sails is turbulent.

Planet

To dream you are on another planet can be interpreted as possibly being out of touch with reality—of not being earthed.

However, if a specific planet is dreamed of then it is to the astrological connotations that you should look for possible meanings:

✦ Mercury represents communication

✦ Venus is the planet of love

✦ Mars represents warlike attributes and aggressiveness

✦ Jupiter symbolises leadership and generosity

✦ Saturn stands for conservation and slow progress

✦ Uranus embodies the quality of thoughtfulness

✦ Neptune represents psychic attributes

✦ Pluto symbolises the spiritual quest.

Police

A dream involving police usually refers to the forces of law and order in your life.

It can also refer to your conscience.

Calling the police for help may indicate you feel helpless and want someone to step in and set things right, or it may suggest you are out of control and need to call on your basic sense of right and wrong to establish order again.

Many police in a dream could mean you are overly conscious of doing the right thing and not allowing your true emotions to have their way.

Feeling guilty in a dream around the police can reflect a fear of being found out for some error of wrongdoing.

Poverty

To dream of poverty can symbolise a fear of actual poverty and overwhelming money concerns in real life, but more than likely it suggests a more general feeling of inadequacy in the self.

Pregnancy

A dream of pregnancy can have interpretations linked to the body or to the creative self.

If the dreamer is pregnant this emotion-charged period of life will power many dreams.

Anxiety, fear and hopes can be played out in pregnancy dreams—all the things you won't let yourself think about when awake will surface in the night.

However, if the dreamer is not pregnant or trying to conceive, this dream suggests the germination and growth of ideas.

A new and still fragile relationship can be symbolised by the developing foetus.

Prince, Princess

The figure of the same sex as the dreamer can represent conscious qualities, while the figure of the opposite sex can symbolise opposite qualities to which you aspire.

Engaging with the prince or princess in the dream could represent how you integrate strong yet opposing elements of your psyche.

If the figure offers a gift, the dream is reminding you of the inner strength and richness you can draw on in times of trouble.

Prize

To be a prize winner in a dream can suggest a hard-won victory.

If you have put effort into solving a problem or rising to a challenge in your personal or professional life, the prize represents not only the positive outcome, but also the strength you have discovered within yourself along the way.

Puncture

This can be a symbol of feeling let down, of disappointment or even grief if you feel something has punctured right through to your heart. There could be a delay on your journey as a result, and frustrations may result.

Alternatively, the dream may be letting you know that in some aspect of your life you need to let the pressure down— a puncture, after all, is less dangerous than a blow-out.

Q

Quadrangle

A square is a symbol of balance and stability, so a quadrangle can represent your feelings of security and being grounded. School associations are important to the interpretation also, as positive memories of the quadrangle can mean that all feels well, while negative ones might suggest restriction, and being hemmed in.

Quarrel

To dream of quarrelling with a figure of the same sex can suggest disruptions in your own psyche—disparate forces in your conscious mind that are pulling in opposite directions.

Quarrelling with a family member or work colleague may be a compensatory dream for everything being fine on the surface—it may be your spirit pointing out to you that all is not well and something needs to be addressed.

Queen

This figure in a dream may represent your ruling passions or the influence in your life of your mother.

It can also represent your spiritual self in a position of ruling power.

If the Queen is someone you recognise this person might be someone who has an influence over you, for better or worse.

Queue

Waiting in a queue can symbolise a sense that at work or in a relationship you are not getting what you want quickly enough.

Alternatively, the dream may be reminding you that all things come in good time and that the discipline of queuing will not go astray.

The queue may also be a play on the letter Q, which stands for 'Question', suggesting you are caught up in a puzzle which you as yet have no answer for.

Quicksand

The awful sensation of being bogged then sucked slowly down in quicksand is a dream symbol of how you feel in your private or professional life. All your efforts seem to be achieving nothing or indeed making things worse.

Another interpretation is that your emotions are overwhelming you and you need to be grounded in order to regain control.

Q

Quilt

The symbolism of sewing or stitching can be seen in a dream of a quilt, but it also has connotations of warmth and maternal love.

A patchwork quilt can suggest the dreamer has pieced together many different parts of life or brought together a variety of qualities and emotions to produce a harmonious whole.

A quilt that does not keep you warm may indicate a lack of love in a relationship, false promises, or a negative maternal influence.

Quiz

Like a dream about an exam, a quiz dream can bring to the surface feelings of being judged, questioned in your worth or of having to tackle a difficult question in your life.

The outcome of the quiz influences its interpretation—if you answer correctly you feel prepared to face the test, but if you fail, or are ill prepared, perhaps there is some homework you need to do.

R

Rabbit

One meaning of a rabbit appearing in your dreams may be that fertility and fecundity are important issues you.
It may also refer to the multiplication of problems in your life.

Rabbits can be seen as cute but vulnerable and perhaps some aspect of your current situation has you feeling that someone is making 'a bunny' out of you.

Hunting rabbits with little success in the dream may indicate that certain elements of your life are frustrating you because you feel you should be able to conquer them but time and again they avoid being pinned down.

A pet rabbit might symbolise that you feel some deep need for gentle, soft nurturing.

Race

The competitive nature inherent in a race of some kind can suggest there is pressure on you to perform and your results will be compared with others.

Judgement and criticism may also be indicated.

A foot race suggests some assessment of the course of your life—does it measure up compared to your own or others' standards?

A race involving bicycles or cars may indicate you are competing for sexual favours in a relationship or that you feel you have to prove your sexual prowess.

Radioactive

To dream of radioactive material can indicate you feel something in your circumstances is contaminating you in a sinister way with effects which could be all pervasive and long lasting.

It is a warning to look at your life or yourself and consider what might need weeding out.

Railway station

A station is the starting point for a journey in waking life and so in a dream it can indicate you are beginning a new stage of our life's journey.

A train journey, however, indicates something undertaken with others, and along expected or predictable lines. This is not a dangerous expedition or wild adventure, but nonetheless it is a new beginning.

To miss the train and have to wait at the station may suggest you missed or are afraid of missing this opportunity.

Being left on the station while your spouse or friend departs in the train may be a warning of an impending separation or at least putting into images your own deepest fears.

A train journey can also, in rare cases, be a symbol of death.

Rain

Traditionally, rain is a sign of cleansing and blessing—to dream of it can suggest the outlet or release of tension and stifled emotion, to good effect.

It may also suggest that after a period of dryness, or purely intellectual communication, a relationship has been blessed by an outpouring of emotion.

Being caught without an umbrella or raincoat may mean the rain feels somewhat annoying or threatening. This is a minor difficulty, even if uncomfortable.

A dream of a sudden rain shower can indicate that in your professional life a new idea has broken through and many benefits can come from it.

R

Rape

This disturbing kind of dream can be interpreted as trauma revisited, fears expressed or a dramatic dream message about abuse in a relationship. Someone you know may be violating your rights and integrity.

Anxiety about entering a sexual relationship may also surface in such a dream.

Rat

Despite connotations of filth or dirt, the rat can symbolise cleverness and survival.

If the rat does not disgust you it is a dream guide to tapping into those qualities you have of endurance and survival cunning.

Another less positive interpretation indicates the presence of something repulsive that feeds on rubbish in your life—an addiction to gossip is one possibility.

Rats in a dream can also indicate something is scurrying about just beneath your conscious understanding and that with a little patience you can trap it and discover its true nature.

If something is gnawing away at you in your waking life, this can be represented by a dream of rats.

Razor

Associated with the cutting edge, whether intellectual, as in a sharp intellect, or emotional, a razor can indicate your sharp tongue and its ability to wound deeply.

To dream of being slashed or cut with a razor might signify someone with a keen mind has seen through your façade.

You doing the cutting can indicate you are not content with accepting the surface that is being presented to you in some aspect of your life, be it work, home or otherwise, and that your insight will seek out the deeper truth.

Refrigerator

A cool-room or refrigerator might suggest sexual frigidity or general emotional coldness in the relationship closest to you.

Another possible meaning can be that you have put something—a project or plan—on ice for the time being and it will keep until the time is right.

It may also suggest there is something in your life you wish to preserve and so prolong its enjoyment.

Revolution

To dream of a social uprising can indicate you have concerns of a negative response to some action that is outside the norm.

Alternatively, it may be your conscience rebelling against actions which betray your true values.

A further interpretation may be that some major upheaval is about to happen in your personal or professional life—the order of things will never be the same.

Revolutions as complete turnings of the wheel may represent the end of a cycle or the completion of a phase in your life.

Ring

The ring as a traditional symbol of betrothal and love can symbolise feelings of commitment in a relationship or to an important project.

A ring falling from the finger may reflect uneasiness regarding the depth of commitment.

A lost ring can indicate trouble in a relationship, infidelity or divorce, which may be conscious or still to surface.

Alternatively, it may suggest the closing of a cycle, the end of a stage in your life.

A ring through the nose can indicate a feeling of being led along by another's will and wishes.

River

A river, as a body of water that is moving to a destination, suggests the course of emotions that are currently carrying you along.

If you cross the river this can indicate you are navigating those emotions successfully and as a result changes are occurring in your life.

If the river is in flood you may be experiencing emotions that threaten to overflow.

Falling into or drowning in a river may suggest a similar predicament.

A river which changes its course can reflect a major change in your feelings about someone or something, while a dried up riverbed suggests aridity in the heart.

The river Styx in mythology was the border between this life and the afterlife, and a ferryman came to carry the souls across from one bank to the next. Thus, on rare occasions, dreaming of a river crossing may suggest death. If you are on one side of the river and a loved one is on the far side this suggests separation through death.

Road

Similar to a path, the dream symbol of a road suggests the direction you are taking in your life.

Driving along the road suggests purpose and control.

Walking can indicate you are enjoying the journey, or alternatively, you are frustrated because things are not progressing fast enough.

A crowded road may indicate difficulty in finding your unique place in the flow of traffic, while a deserted road may suggest you feel alone in the direction you have chosen to take.

A twisting turning road can symbolise many variations in your focus while a steep road with obstacles reflects the feeling that the way you are going is a difficult one.

Robot

As you might expect, the robot symbolises a mechanical approach to life.

You actually being the robot can suggest you are acting out of habit, without any creativity or purpose.

If you are surrounded by robots in the dream perhaps you feel yourself the only free thinking individual in your social or work environment.

The metal suit of the robot can also suggest armour and the ability to withstand attack and stay focussed on an objective.

Ruins

A dream about wandering among ruins may symbolise memories or a past that is irretrievable.

Alternatively such can suggest a relationship or important project is ruined.

If the ruins are peaceful there is acceptance that the past is gone and the new has replaced it.

If the ruins are smoking, perhaps some trauma has brought to an end a phase of your life.

Rust

A symbol of decay, rust can suggest something eating away at the dreamer.

Even an iron will can be broken down if the conditions

are right. Rust requires water and so the presence of emotions is indicated.

The red stain of rust is also very hard to remove and may represent guilt or shame.

S

Sacrifice

The symbol of a sacrifice in a dream can reflect how you are feeling about your role in a relationship or work situation.

If you are making the sacrifice in the dream, this could suggest you feel you have been required to give up something you value—a pastime, other friendships or personal values –to ensure everything goes smoothly.

If you are the sacrifice, the dream may be telling you the cost of some action or venture you are about to undertake is too high.

Saint

To encounter a saint in a dream is traditionally interpreted as a meeting with the spiritual aspects of your psyche—a healing union.

The saint embodies collective wisdom and enlightenment regarding eternal things.

For those who follow Christianity, many saints are associated with specific aspects of life, such as medicine, pets, occupations or qualities, and thus further understanding can be gained by identifying these associations and applying them to your dream.

Sand

Sand, as an irritant and an abrasive, is most often interpreted literally as just this.

However, if you are walking upon sand in your dream, as the meeting place of land and water this can suggest a transition period, usually involving strong emotions.

Sand in your clothes in a dream can indicate some aspects of your social personality need refining or are causing abrasion in your relationships.

The sands of time represent the fleeting nature of life, and so pouring sand in a dream might be a reminder time is running out.

Satan

In Western religion, Satan is seen as the embodiment of evil and so to encounter this symbol in a dream can reflect the dreamer's fears or unconscious knowledge.

The perceived 'evil' may be external, as in a person of bad influence, or may be urges and passions within you. If strong negative or sexual emotions are claiming you, the figure of Satan may represent these.

S

Scarf

As with the necktie, the symbol of a scarf focuses on the throat and so can relate to issues of speech or breathing.

A scarf tied too tight could suggest the dreamer feels voiceless or unable to breath in a current situation. Perhaps you are feeling you can't communicate, or if another person is wearing the scarf, perhaps you do not trust what they say.

Anther interpretation is that health issues may be implied.

A scarf worn on the head may suggest shame about sexuality.

School

Dreams about a school in our past are common because we continue to learn all through life.

The symbol generally refers to a learning situation and, depending on the feelings associated in waking life with school, can suggest positive or negative things.

If school was an unhappy experience for you, to dream of it can indicate you feel misunderstood, belittled and powerless in the current situation. The focus of the dream however can be varied. If it is concerned with being late for class, the main issue before you may be the timing of this life lesson—are you too late to change and adapt?

If the dream is set in the schoolyard, the social aspects—positive and negative—of your current learning situation are highlighted.

The appearance of a favourite teacher in a dream is possibly an indication you are your own best teacher and the learning you are doing will benefit you.

School uniforms can suggest external rules that are no longer appropriate to your adult life. School sports suggest competitiveness in your current learning—a feeling of having to perform better than others to make the grade.

Scissors

Using scissors in a dream can be a symbol of severing connections.

It can also be interpreted as referring to the tongue, which can cut with cruel comments.

If in the dream your clothes are cut with scissors perhaps someone has said something that destroys your reputation.

Sex

Sexual activity in a dream may be an outworking of physical frustrations or desires.

Such dreams are extremely common as often what is not permitted in the waking world is released in sleep. This is the natural compensation of the body.

However, there are other interpretations, which include a union of opposing forces within the psyche or an imbalance if one of the partners in the dream is aggressive and the other submissive.

Shadow

As with dreams of darkness, the shadow in a dream can indicate things obscure or unknown.

It is usually attached to a body and thus can symbolise the unconscious mind.

Shoes

The traditional interpretation of shoes is that they reflect the dreamer's 'standing' in life.

If the shoes are dirty perhaps you feel you have dropped in the regard of your colleagues.

A sports shoe might suggest you feel ready to take on new challenges to raise your standing.

Losing your shoes and going barefoot in a dream can suggest exposure.

If financial issues are pressing on you, this could be a warning.

Shop

Like the marketplace symbol, a shop is a place of transaction. The wares on display can represent your opportunities in life.

If you bargain or are looking for cheap goods this may suggest some part of you is not willing to pay the price or exert the required effort in life.

An empty shop can be a symbol of your feeling that life has nothing to offer them and can sometimes indicate depression.

Silver

As a precious metal, silver can suggest spiritual values in a dream.

It may also suggest relationships held dear or precious

memories, especially if the dream object is antique.

Silver has associations with age and wisdom, and also with optimism.

Sleep

To dream of being asleep may symbolise there is something in your life you are not awake to, or an opportunity or a problem that needs your attention.

It can also indicate you feel 'out of it' in a personal or professional situation.

Another figure sleeping can indicate you feel that person should wake up to what is in front of them.

Alternatively, it may suggest it is time you let that person or problem go—to let sleeping dogs lie.

Snake

The snake is the classical symbol of the sex drive and thus can represent the penis.

If you are handling the snake this can mean you are facing sexual temptation.

If your partner is handling a snake, a possible interpretation is that you suspect they are having an affair.

Although in our society snakes are often feared, in other cultures they are revered and given god-like status. The snake can thus represent eternity and spiritual wisdom.

A negative interpretation is that of a snake in the

grass—sabotage. Killing a snake in this situation has the clear meaning you will gain victory of treachery that exists somewhere in your life.

If the snake bites you this may suggest sexual activity will have negative results.

Spider

Entrapment is a common theme in interpreting spider dreams. Perhaps you feel someone is lying in wait to catch you or that you are associating with someone who has the potential to suck your emotions.

If the spider terrifies you this can indicate sexual disgust, especially relating to the female sex organs, or you may feel that a woman is trying to trap you through sex.

In some cultures the spider is considered wise and can represent patience and knowledge of history and the future.

A spider may also symbolise the number eight and therefore eternity.

Stairs

Stairs in a dream usually indicate you are facing a challenge and must rise to the occasion. It will be important to keep your balance and take measured steps.

A staircase may represent the opportunity to move to a higher spiritual plane or to take on study and gain higher understanding.

A staircase in a house can suggest the link between physical or natural urges and the intellect.

Falling through stairs can indicate you are afraid you will not achieve the goals you have set.

Storm

Wind, rain, thunder and lightning in a dream are associated with a violent outpouring of emotions. Perhaps you have been the victim of this or it could be a warning that unless feelings are given a regulated outlet, this destruction will come from you.

Taking shelter from a storm can indicate someone or something in your life will help you through.

Your house being destroyed by a storm may indicate physical damage, such as self-harm or an accident, which could result from pent-up anger.

If you are struggling to reach an agreement on something this may indicate a desire to barge through and overwhelm the opposition.

Sun

In mythology the sun is the life force, the symbol of God.

Joy and knowledge are also symbolised by this great source of light and so to dream of the sun may refer to knowledge gained or a state of happiness.

To be drawn to the sun in a dream can suggest spiritual enlightenment or religious desire. To go too close to the sun can indicate pride and suggests that a fall is imminent because your wings will melt as with the famous myth of Icarus.

The sun, as a word that sounds the same as 'son', may also represent your own son, if you have one.

Clouds covering the sun's face might suggest worries or health problems facing your child.

Surfing

To be surfing in a dream can symbolise the dreamer's ability to ride the waves of emotion in their life.

It can also represent a oneness with nature, especially the sea.

A sexual interpretation is that the dreamer is enjoying the surges of sexual desire and the act itself, and feels confident in sexual situations.

T

Table

A dream set around a kitchen table can suggest family matters or kin relationships.

Being around a work table or boardroom table may have associations to issues of productivity—it is most often a symbol of the everyday actions and responsibilities that uphold your job or family life.

If the table is bare you may feel a responsibility to put something on it—to make a suggestion or proposal.

Dining at a table can refer to the type of nourishment you feel you are receiving from family.

Tail

Dreaming that you have a tail can symbolise the carrying around of something unnecessary from the past and a need to put it behind you. This may be a vestigial or leftover value or attitude, especially one relating to sex.

An alternate meaning can be that it is an expression of the primitive sexual drive, which, like a tail, links us to the animals.

Tail wagging is a form of communication, and so this image can mean you feel a strong need to communicate.

A similar meaning is that it is a homonym for the word 'tale' and so can refer to a story that the dreamer wants to tell, perhaps surprising news.

Tall

To dream you have extra height usually suggests pride and a sense of superiority.

If others in your dream are significantly taller than you, the meaning may be that you are feeling overshadowed by those around you and a little insignificant.

To grow during the course of a dream may reflect rapid development of confidence at this period in the dreamer's life.

Tap

A tap in a dream can symbolise tears and hence sadness.

Turning on a tap may suggest you feel a need to cry but repress the emotion.

Turning the tap off can indicate a deliberate choice to cut off the flow of emotions—control of expression of feeling is indicated.

Another interpretation is that tap is a pun for the sound of knocking (also reminiscent of the dripping sound a tap can make if left on) and in this scenario the tap may symbolise your fear of receiving bad news.

Tapestry

A tapestry is a big picture made from small stitches, a metaphor for the story of your life.

Tapestries traditionally relate important events—stitching a tapestry in your dream may suggest you are consciously reflecting on the events in your life and putting them together to shape some understanding of your destiny.

Others stitching the tapestry might indicate you are aware that what you do is being watched, perhaps by your children or your parents.

It can also mean you feel that someone else is pulling the strings or holding the threads of your life.

Target

There are many possible interpretations of a target and they depend upon the feelings in the dream and the location of the target.

If you are wearing a bulls-eye the obvious interpretation is of feelings of being targeted.

Firing at a bulls-eye or other target may suggest concentration upon a goal and determination to reach it.

T

The circles of the bulls-eye target may also suggest wheels within wheels or a complex problem.

Tattoo

A tattoo in a dream can suggest some experience that has gotten beneath your skin and left a permanent mark.

The design of the dream tattoo will be your guide as to the nature of this experience—for example, a love-heart or dove is positive; skull and crossbones would suggest something painful, even life-threatening.

If others in the dream are also wearing tattoos this might suggest a feeling of having been initiated into a new social circle.

Teacher

To dream of a teacher from your school days suggests you are once again in a learning situation in your waking life.

If the teacher was a favourite, the learning may be going well and benefiting you, while a bullying teacher can refer to feelings of having to learn something you would rather not learn.

The learning may be practical, emotional or spiritual, and so the nature of the teacher will be your guide to interpretation.

If the teacher approaches you from the distance, this can indicate it is time you learned a lesson and your inner resources are coming to your aid.

Teeth

Sometimes a dream of losing teeth is interpreted to mean death in the family but there are many other meanings to this symbol.

To grow new teeth can suggest you have found a way to add some bite in a competitive environment.

False teeth may refer to feelings of deception in a close relationship.

The snapping of teeth can mean the making of decisions, perhaps abruptly.

A bad or rotten tooth might indicate something has been said that is spreading pain and poison through your family or yourself.

To be toothless in a dream might suggest you feel weak in situations where some strong words are necessary.

Telephone

If you are on the telephone in a dream and can't hear the voice of the person you are speaking to, this points towards you being out of touch with a particular subject.

When it is you who cannot speak, this is likely to mean you may have nothing to say about a particular matter in your life or someone else's life that is affecting yours, or that you lack the skill to say something.

The telephone also brings with it, for those who believe in such, the notion of a telepathic message or spiritual communication.

Telegram

On rare occasions, to dream of a telegram arriving is precognition of bad news about to reach you.

However, just as a telegram in waking life would more objectively suggest, it is more commonly a symbol of receiving or imparting important information.

Tent

An impermanent dwelling, the tent in a dream can symbolise a state of transition or impermanence in your domestic situation, or in your health situation.

Camping out in a dream may suggest a need to make contact with nature or your natural impulses—to let things go wild for a time.

Alternatively, it may be a reminder that you need to get back to basics.

Termite

To dream of termites can indicate anxieties about being 'white anted'—perhaps some project has been sabotaged from within.

Issues surrounding health may also be suggested.

Another meaning can be that worries are riddling your life, eroding your strength and threatening to cause collapse.

Sometimes, if no negative feelings are involved, termites can simply suggest your life is a hive of activity and that great industry surrounds you.

Tiger

Tigers are associated with power and can indicate the commencement of a phase in your life where you will overcome opposition and rise to a high position, allowing you to enjoy luxuries you have not hitherto known.

They also signify wild beauty and intense sexual force, generally from a masculine perspective.

Tongue

As an organ of communication, the tongue in dreams usually represents feelings about your ability to make yourself understood.

A tongue that has been cut out may suggest you feel silenced.

An overlong tongue can suggest gossip or invasive talking.

Another interpretation of a long tongue is sexual—it can mimic the limp penis.

Train

Trains can symbolise many things, although Freud would immediately suggest they are phallic and thus have a sexual overtone.

If you are travelling in one compartment and do not

have access to others this might suggest your life is overly compartmentalised and that there is not much communication between the various parts.

A steam train can indicate built up emotions in one or all of these areas or can be interpreted to mean nostalgic memories.

A freight train can indicate you may be carrying a lot of luggage around with you, your own or others.

As a pun, the concept of a train might suggest teaching skills and if you are driving this train, this interpretation could particularly apply.

Tree

The tree is a common symbol in dreams, ancient art and religion.

Classically it symbolises the self concept, or even God.

It can also be a symbol for the life force or for your family heritage.

The type and condition of the tree can shed further light on understanding its meaning—decay, new shoots, peeled bark, fruit, broken branches, nests in the limbs, and lightning scars all have clear meanings.

If you are perched high in a tree in a dream this can suggest you are aspiring to great heights or that you have been elevated in the eyes of your family because you have been true to your background and kept your roots.

Falling from a tree can suggest a schism in the psyche, but more likely ostracism from your family.

Turtle

As an animal that has a soft body but a hard shell, the turtle in a dream can symbolise your sense of self-preservation.

Slow deliberate movements are also symbolised and this may be a message from your dream spirit to take things very carefully—to make no hasty decisions.

Turtles also have the ability to pull their heads in, so another interpretation is that in a current situation you may be wishing you could retreat a little, and wait while the crisis passes.

UFO

A space ship in a dream can suggest contact with distant or alien parts of yourself.

It can also suggest you are open to different perspectives on your life or that you are in communion with your own spiritual nature.

Circles and light in such a dream reinforce the symbolism of wisdom and eternity.

If fear or terror is involved, the visitation may symbolise invasion into your life of alien values or ways of doing things.

Underclothes

Appearing in public in your underclothes may suggest your fear of people discovering what is beneath your external appearance.

Alternatively, it may be wish fulfilment—a desire to reveal deeper layers of yourself.

Dirty underclothes can suggest guilt about undiscovered 'crimes' or mistakes.

Lacy lingerie can have connotations of romance or indicate you believe yourself beautiful underneath.

Undertaker

A possible interpretation of the appearance of an undertaker in your dream is that something in your life has died and must be taken away and buried. This may be a relationship, a way of doing things, or a stage of your life such as rearing small children.

If grief is associated with the undertaker in the dream you may be feeling sad about letting go, but if you feel no sadness, you are happily moving on.

As a pun, the undertaker may represent you starting out on a new 'undertaking'.

Underwater

To be submerged in a dream suggests 'going under' your own emotions—if there is panic, the feelings may be overwhelming you.

If you have breathing apparatus, or find you can breathe naturally in the water, this can be taken as a reminder that you can survive this emotional time.

Discovering life forms in the water can suggest spiritual reflection.

Unicorn
A mythical, fantastic beast, the unicorn traditionally protects virgins and so its appearance in a dream can reflect the dreamer's fears surrounding losing virginity, whether this is a past event or one not yet experienced.

It can symbolise honourable love and courtly romance and so can be a wish fulfilment dream.

Unicorns are traditionally almost impossible to catch and so they may also suggest you have wonderful fantasies that elude the grasp of reality.

Uniform
To dream of yourself in uniform can be a symbol of feeling pressure to conform.

If others are in uniform, but you are not, it may indicate you feel everyone else is thinking along the same lines while you are the odd one out.

U

Valley
A valley in a dream can be a symbol of things being in a slump in your life or of depression or sadness.

Alternatively, a valley can be a place protected from the winds and so this may suggest a peaceful hiatus in your life.

If the valley is rich and green, fertility is suggested.

As a sexual symbol, the valley can refer to the female organs, especially if it has a narrow entrance such as through a chasm.

Vampire

Vampires can refer to your feelings of being leeched or bled dry by others. This can be emotional or financial, or even refer to someone who is draining all your energy with their demands.

If you are the vampire, this can symbolise your need to feed off others' ideas or activities to make yourself feel nourished.

Volcano

A symbol of destruction and eruption, the volcano suggests an overflow of red hot emotions and its resulting damage. You may be feeling that emotions have been bottled up for so long that something is about to blow.

Surviving an eruption in a dream can indicate that, despite the passion and anger involved, things will go on.

Vulture

Far from being a disgusting creature, the vulture recycles naturally and is also responsible for keeping the environment free of disease.

Thus, a dream of vultures may not necessarily have connotations of impending death. It can symbolise regeneration, change or new beginnings.

Alternatively, you may feel that others are stealing life from you, feeding off your creativity or generosity.

Warehouse

Generally understood to symbolise the storehouse of memory, a warehouse in a dream may indicate you are searching through your past for clues to the present.

It can also symbolise all your skills and knowledge and so can suggest you are drawing upon these in a current demanding situation.

An empty warehouse can reflect the dreamer's fear about memory loss or lost skills.

Pulling things out of storage can suggest you are accessing interests or skills which have been put on hold for some time while you did something else in your life.

Warrior

The warrior or soldier can be a symbol of your inner aggression and so can be negative if not disciplined, but it may also suggest your defensive attitude to life or a current situation.

A defeated warrior may mean you have soothed your aggressive urges or that you feel a battle has been lost.

Washing

The action of washing can symbolise a sense of purification and cleansing, linked possibly to guilt.

Washing hands repeatedly may represent guilt over past actions and a desire to be cleansed.

Washing clothes can indicate you wanting to present a

cleaner image to the world.

Wasp

To be stung in a dream by a wasp is usually an indication you have suffered criticism that has caused pain.

Revenge and spitefulness are other interpretations.

Wealth

Riches in a dream suggest a sense of well-being and faith in life. The riches may represent your family, a love relationship, professional satisfaction or creative achievement.

Wealth gained by illegal means in a dream, or stolen from another, can suggest that feelings of satisfaction and bounty are not based upon solid foundations.

Whale

Sighting a whale in your dreams is a positive sign of power and strength, and generally that good times are coming.

Whales are also a sign that there is a great truth of some kind you are finally able and ready to accept.

A beached whale, or one that is captured or injured, should be considered carefully as a sign that some great plans you have or current good times are threatened in some way.

Whisper

Whispering in the background of a dream can indicate you are aware of gossip behind your back.

If you are whispering, it may indicate a desire for more privacy.

If the whispering frustrates you, this can suggest you feel

unable to express your opinions strongly.

Wind

Change is generally symbolised by wind.

A gentle breeze can suggest you are experiencing small subtle changes in your life.

A violent gale suggests destructive and unsought change, such as the breakdown of a relationship or loss of a job.

Wine

Wine, as a symbol of shared social events and celebration, can indicate you need to celebrate some aspect of yourself—an achievement or a challenge successfully negotiated.

Spilt wine can mean wastefulness.

As a religious symbol, the wine represents the blood of Christ and so may also suggest a sacrifice.

Write

To write in a dream may indicate you have given careful thought to some issue and now wish to explain yourself in clear terms—it is a symbol of measured self-expression.

It can also be a pun on the word 'right' and so has the double meaning that the dreamer feels the need to communicate what they consider right.

Writing appearing in the dream of its own accord can

be a message that the writing is on the wall and the truth is about to come out.

X

The letter 'X'

As the symbol of the unknown quantity, something marked with an X in a dream can suggest that it is not what it appears.

A person wearing clothing with criss-cross patterns might also be concealing the truth about their nature, or at least you may believe this.

X can also indicate buried treasure, so a person in a dream wearing an X might be offering you hidden 'jewels', whether they be of the physical, emotional or spiritual kind.

X-ray

To have an x-ray taken in a dream might suggest you feel under close scrutiny in some aspect of your personal or professional life.

It might also indicate a feeling that someone can see right through you and further deception is not possible.

Yet a further interpretation is that of an invasion of privacy.

To be studying x-rays can reflect a commitment to get to the core of a problem and not be satisfied with what presents upon the surface.

Yellow

As the colour associated with cowardice in Western culture, its prevalence in a dream may refer to this element in a dreamer's life.

However it is also the colour of the sun, of summer bounty, and so can symbolise health and energy.

Youth

Energy, unfinished potential, openness and flexibility are suggested by the figure of a youth in a dream.

There is also a suggestion that you may be on the verge or cusp of something.

If you are an adult and dream of yourself as a youth again, this can refer to a feeling of enthusiasm and excitement regarding a new relationship or project.

It can suggest good health and a sense of vitality.

Z

Zero

As an ovoid shape, the numeral zero in a dream can represent the feminine, creative aspects of the dreamer.

As a place holder in the world of mathematics, it wields great power and so may represent in a dream your personal sense of exerting power without having to make a great show of it, or marking time in waiting.

If frustrations surround the zero, this may indicate the wait should soon be over—that 'zero hour' has arrived.

Zero can also represent spiritual poverty.

Zoo

To visit a zoo in a dream can represent a visit to the unconscious or animal urges—just as zoo animals are contained, so too are these aspects of the dreamer.

However, a breakout from the zoo can warn of the potential for escape of untamed aspects of the psyche.

Attention to the types of animals in the dream zoo will aid interpretation.

Also available from Brolga Publishing

More Sayings of the Buddha
by Mark Zocchi
RRP $15.99 • ISBN 9781921221781

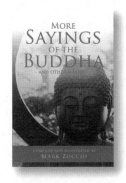

Bring joy, be inspired or find your divinity
while flicking through and absorbing the
words of wisdom that great masters like
Sogyal Rinpoche and the 14th Dalai Lama
have to offer. Quotes, sayings
and insights are complimented by
watercolour illustrations.

The Little Prince
by Antoine de Saint Exupéry
RRP $9.99 • ISBN 9781921596162

When a pilot finds himself alone and
stranded with a broken-down plane, a little
prince is his only companion living on a
strange deserted planet. First published in
1943 and written by now-famous French
writer Antoine de Saint Exupéry, this is a
timeless classic for all ages.

		QTY
Dream Dictionary	$19.99	....
More Sayings of the Buddha	$15.99	....
The Little Prince	$ 9.99	....
Postage within Australia	$ 6.00	....

TOTAL* $_____

* All prices include GST

Name: ....

Address: ....

Phone: ....

Email Address: ....

Payment:

❑ Money Order ❑ Cheque ❑ Amex ❑ MasterCard ❑ Visa

Cardholder's Name: ....

Credit Card Number: _ _ _ _ - _ _ _ _ - _ _ _ _ - _ _ _ _

Signature:...

Expiry Date: _ _ / _ _

Allow 21 days for delivery.

Payment to: Better Bookshop (ABN 14 067 257 390)
PO Box 12544
A'Beckett Street, Melbourne, 8006
Victoria, Australia
betterbookshop@brolgapublishing.com.au

BE PUBLISHED

Publishing through a successful Australian publisher. Brolga provides:

- Editorial appraisal
- Cover design
- Typesetting
- Printing
- Author promotion
- National book trade distribution, including sales, marketing and distribution through Macmillan Australia.

For details and inquiries, contact:
Brolga Publishing Pty Ltd
PO Box 12544
A'Beckett St VIC 8006

bepublished@brolgapublishing.com.au
markzocchi@brolgapublishing.com.au
ABN: 46 063 962 443